NEW
WEBSTER'S

SECRETARY'S
& STUDENT'S
GUIDE

AVENEL BOOKS   NEW YORK

NEW
WEBSTER'S

SECRETARY'S
& STUDENT'S
GUIDE

Contents

CONTENTS

CONTENTS

Chapter 1

THE SUCCESSFUL SECRETARY

The Secretarial Position

The secretary acts as a personal representative, responsible for accurately conveying information to her employer and accurately issuing his communications and instructions. The activities of the secretary may vary greatly from employer to employer, sometimes involving only intelligent execution of instructions and in other instances demanding considerable initiative and judgment, but the elements of tact and mediation are always apparent. This is inevitable in the modern world, where the interrelationships between business and public, and between business and business, are constantly developing new ramifications. The present-day secretary plays an important role, and upon her efficiency depends much of the smooth functioning of the executive.

This does not imply that the secretary has superseded the executive, notwithstanding fictional or actual instances to the contrary. Most employers consider themselves competent to do their own thinking, and often resent any but the most subtly phrased of unsolicited or solicited suggestions, although they are quick to appreciate all assistance that lightens their tasks without challenging their authority. Secretaries who think for their employers, functioning as a kind of master mind behind a screen, are largely a product of twentieth-century fiction. The competent executive's appetite for argument and advice is usually well satisfied by conference with his colleagues and clients.

ACCURACY

One of the most important qualifications of a proficient secretary is accuracy. It insures the employer against having to check and recheck small items in search of possible errors. It gives him a comfortable feeling of security. If he has someone he can trust, he need not clog his mind with detail.

Accuracy is more a matter of self-discipline than education. A person widely read and highly educated may frequently be guilty of inaccuracies in his thinking and in the oral or written expression of his thoughts, particularly if he makes a point of glibly rattling off answers to all questions in order to create an impression of brilliance and encyclopedic knowledge. The really accurate individual makes a very clear distinction between facts of which he is certain and notions about which he is vague or doubtful. He has schooled himself to trust and employ the former, and not to waste time trying to puzzle out the latter, especially when consultation of some recognized authority would quickly resolve his doubts.

UNREASONABLE WORRY

Accuracy, however, need not and should not involve constant recourse to authorities, whether they be books, persons, or information agencies. Such recourse can become a pernicious habit, subtly undermining the individual's confidence in his every belief and assertion, until the spelling of the simplest word or the recalling of the most familiar telephone number awakens overwhelming doubts. The competent secretary does not let such unreasonable worries get the upper hand. She not only knows, but she knows that she knows. Moreover, in consulting authorities, she seeks not only to find an answer for the immediate problem, but also, time permitting, to imprint on her own mind the information so gained, provided it seems likely to be useful a second time and is of such a nature as to be readily learned. Such intelligent use of authorities is in itself an education, rapidly building up a skeleton framework of key facts, into which further information can easily be inserted. Knowledge, if so organized, begets knowledge, since interrelated facts provide clues to each other, and are much more easily recalled than isolated facts.

FRAMEWORK

It is difficult to exaggerate the importance for the secretary of such a skeleton framework, including such fields as spelling, grammar, and usage; frequently used addresses and telephone numbers; recognized forms of letters; proper methods of indexing and filing; regulations on mailing and shipping; the names and faces of individuals and their personality, occupation, and degree of importance; office procedure both general and specific; and arrangement of interviews and appointments. The executive, specialist, or scholar can and very often should forget matters of detail in order to devote his mind more completely and effectively to larger issues. Indeed, it is for this very reason that he employs a secretary. He desires to be left with as free a hand as possible and depends on his secretary to handle all minor matters with intelligence, decision, and discretion. This division of labor, when properly carried out by both parties, is a very effective one.

MATTERS OF DETAIL

The secretary should never, unless it is absolutely unavoidable, question the employer on matters of detail. Such questioning amounts to a confession that she doesn't know her job, and is especially irritating to the employer because it forces him to think about the very problems of which he wishes to be relieved.

SECRETARY-STENOGRAPHER

In matters of knowledge and accuracy the requirements of the stenographer are similar to those of the secretary, except that the activities of the former are necessarily limited to a narrower field. Shorthand and typing are usually the sole occupations of the stenographer. To the secretary they are a type of equipment that she is able to use with great facility to accomplish her wider and more varied duties.

The duties of the secretary are not only more complicated and numerous than those of the stenographer; they involve greater responsibility and flexibility, and a significant personal element. The stenographer works with words; the secretary with people. In this connection the quality of restraint or unobtrusiveness, though not preeminent, is especially characteristic and undeniably important.

COMPORTMENT

The successful secretary does not obviously impose her personality on her surroundings, but has a way of shading into the background. She cultivates a soft but distinct voice, a quiet but capable manner. Her style of dressing is pleasing to the eye but usually simple and neat, and, above all, suited to the type of establishment in which she is working. Tact and discretion are habitual to her. She is self-effacing—but never hesitant or shy, for she knows that such tactics are out of place in the office, immediately making her a bother rather than a help. At conferences and interviews she maintains a thoroughly impersonal attitude, which facilitates matters and avoids embarrassment. She manages to do this without appearing bored or aloof.

DISCRETION

The nature of the secretarial functions puts an unusually great premium on discretion and restraint. Inevitably the secretary comes to know a great many matters—many of which are confidential—concerning the firm and employer for whom she is working. Her position as a personal representative makes it dangerously easy for her to pass on private information about her immediate employer to the staff, and about members of the staff to her employer. Both of these activities can easily become unethical and damaging. The accomplished secretary avoids them; by establishing a reputation for discretion, she gains the cooperation of her colleagues. She also makes it possible for her employer to think, talk, plan, and thrash matters out freely, without feeling a need for caution in her presence and a fear of subsequent ridicule. She becomes a kind of business confidant. In so doing, she advances her status greatly and is better able to play the role of trusted assistant, leaving her employer free to consider major problems.

Ease and Efficiency

The personal qualities of a successful secretary cannot be singled out of her personality, for actually they are all interdependent. For example, accuracy, knowledge, self-discipline, and confidence go hand in hand; one cannot exist without at least something of the others. In the successful personality all qualities are well integrated.

The same is true of ease and efficiency. It is difficult to do things easily without doing them efficiently, and it is difficult to be truly efficient if nervous and tense. Naturally, a person cannot relax while learning a new job. At such times the mind is constantly active—learning, experimenting, testing, watching itself for errors. Even at such a time too much tenseness represents energy wasted. Once the groundwork of the job is learned, it is possible to devote more time to doing it smoothly. Matters of routine become a habit, and the mind is free for other considerations.

SURPRISES

In the swiftly changing world of business, surprises are the rule. The secretary, whose tasks are usually so numerous that her work is never done, must be ready to meet all kinds of demands on her time. Correspondence to be read, letters to be typed, incoming and outgoing telephone calls, dictation, arranging of appointments and conferences, inquiries and instructions—all may descend upon her at once. She is expected to handle them all dexterously and without losing her poise.

SHIFTING DUTIES

The proficient secretary is busy but never preoccupied. She shifts smoothly from one job to another without hesitation because she knows which action takes precedence. When the telephone rings, she does not desperately attempt to finish several lines of typing before answering it—nor does she necessarily break off nervously in the middle of a word. By rigorous self-discipline she learns to leave a piece of work in the middle and come back to it with a minimum loss of time. If she is called upon to do so many things at once that she begins to forget some of them—and that can happen to the most skillful secretary—she takes care of the most pressing matters first and then turns her attention to the others.

EFFECTIVE ROUTINE

Such efficiency is largely a matter of following a routine, and an effective and time-saving routine comprises two chief elements: good habits and the ability to make plans. Habit is what enables an individual to perform a task with a minimum of conscious thought. Any action that is repeated sufficiently becomes a habit: walking is a habit; dancing or typing may become habits. Saying "Good morning" to certain individuals and walking down one side of a street rather than another are matters of habit. But not all habits are desirable ones. In learning to use the typewriter, for example, the "hunt and peck" system can become just as habitual as the touch system. A stenographer may learn to consult the dictionary automatically when confronted by an unfamiliar word, but she may also learn to become so dependent on the dictionary as to seriously limit her ability; both are habits. Saying "Hello" when answering the telephone may become a habit, although the word "Hello" is usually a waste of time, since it tells nothing and must be immediately followed by an explanation as to who is saying "Hello." In short, habit alone is not enough. Before allowing any action to become habitual, one should ask, "Is it an efficient and smooth-flowing action, performed in the fewest number of moves? Will it be an asset to my personality, or just an unnecessary burden? Is it a shortcut, or the long way around?" Thoughts, too, can become as habitual as actions: the mind develops its stereotyped patterns, which may be either helps or hindrances. In these matters, every person must be his own efficiency expert. Business and secretarial schools, of course, inculcate in the individual a groundwork of efficient habits, but the work does not end there. Every time a new routine is learned or an old routine is changed, careful thought must be devoted to habit-building. Question each procedure thoroughly as to its advantages and disadvantages.

PLANNING

The ability to make plans—the other element of an effective routine—

demands clear thinking. Every executive has some method of arranging his day's work and that of his secretary. The first hour of the morning may be devoted to reading and answering correspondence; then interviews may be held with members of the staff, followed by interviews with salesmen and other outsiders, each task being handled at a definite time. But there is no such thing as a foolproof and unalterable routine. Interruptions are always coming up. Pressing matters must be given a special time allotment or shoved ahead. The day's routine must be rearranged again and again. Much of the responsibility for such tasks as postponing interviews without hurting feelings, or seeing that essential business is handled by an employer deep in conference, falls on the secretary. To plan a routine calls only for careful deliberation, but to break a routine and replace it with a new one on short notice demands ingenuity and quick thinking.

Dealing with People

The good secretary is well liked. Visitors to the office will recall her courteous, cheerful manner, her intelligent considerateness, and her smile. Fellow employees value her helpful cooperation. As for her employer, he depends on her in a number of ways, not only in business dealings but sometimes in social matters as well. It is part of her job to create a good impression, and to establish and maintain friendly relations.

SMOOTHNESS

The business world moves at high speed. The office building hums with activity. Executives are drawn together by a complex web of letters, telephone calls, conversations, and agreements. Transactions are set under way whose success depends on the swift and efficient functioning of each employee, from the highest to the most subordinate. In this fast-moving world, confusions, misunderstandings, delays, and other manifestations of poor cooperation prove costly. Yet it is all too easy for an individual to develop a hurried, nervous tempo of working, no more efficient than a burst of speed by a high-powered auto in heavy traffic. Obviously, greater smoothness in personal relations and functioning is very important.

MEDIATOR

The secretary is a vital part of this swiftly moving scene and her position enables her to obtain a perspective of the entire picture. Since she is, among other things, a mediator, she is in a good position to help the office function smoothly. She can make it easier for people to cooperate. She can help to keep those with whom she comes in contact in good humor, soften their disappointments, increase their enthusiasm. She can do her best to smooth over difficulties, lessen intraoffice jealousies, and avoid gaining the reputation of gossip and office spy.

The good secretary has developed the qualities of ease and efficiency and is therefore able to relax to a certain degree during her work; by doing this she makes it easier for others to relax. She does not "fight against" her job, wasting time in worry and bitterness, but makes her work a part of her life. She promotes a similarly healthy attitude in others.

PERSONAL RELATIONS

To be able to do all this, the secretary must be an expert at personal relations. A great deal has been written about the art of handling people. Psychologists, authors, homespun philosophers, and "business experts" of varying intelligence and ability have told the world how to "make friends," conciliate enemies, and develop an irresistible personality. Their copious advice can usually be reduced to one central principle: that any human being is somewhat egotistical and likes to feel important. Therefore, he likes the sound of his own name; he likes to be reminded of his success and good points; he likes to be remembered and to feel that people have affection for him; he likes compliments, provided they are not too obviously flattering; he likes to think that his ideas and suggestions receive serious attention. He does not like to remember his failures and failings; he does not like to admit he's wrong or give up an untenable position in an argument, unless there is a graceful "out"; he fears sarcasm; he is jealous of success; and he does not like to be forgotten. All this is, of course, very true, as the secretary who understands anything of human nature is well aware; and she must also know how to make use of this knowledge. However, a human being is more than a self-centered, jealous child, and there is a limit to the use that can be made of methods for handling people by flattery, facile enthusiasm, and general heartiness. Sincerity, courtesy, and unforced human interest—natural rather than artificial qualities—are more important.

EMPLOYER'S HABITS

Another important consideration is that all individuals are different. Each has his own quirks and idiosyncracies. The methods that work with one will not necessarily work with another. The good secretary is a student of individual human nature, and learns more than names and faces and occupations. She discovers the things that please and displease the people with whom she comes in contact; she comes to know their strong and weak points. Above all, she studies the personality of her employer with a concentrated interest. His habits in giving dictation; his attitude toward salesmen; his tendencies to hurry through certain matters and linger over others, are all matters of importance to her. She discovers the extent to which he wishes her to make changes in the form of his letters, or rearrange materials on his desk. This study is for the most part a silent one, conducted by observation rather than questions, yet it is of vital importance. It enables the secretary to handle her work in the way her employer would like to see it handled, and, by adjusting her personality to his, to serve her employer most satisfactorily.

Chapter 2

OFFICE ROUTINE

An effective office routine is based on common sense. It is no different from the routine used by a clear-thinking and efficient individual in his personal affairs, except that it has greater scope and is adapted to the needs of a business and the workers who compose it. An orderly individual makes memoranda of approaching tasks and appointments; keeps a careful watch on bills, checks, and bank statements; files away important letters, documents, and receipts in such a fashion that he can find them again easily; makes careful plans before traveling; and in general tries to dispatch the business of life with a minimum of bother and error. The same is true of an efficient office. Time is a precious commodity, and hours saved can be devoted effectively to more important efforts.

REASONABLE ROUTINE

This does not mean that all office routines are perfect. In some there is the hampering red tape and "system for system's sake." In others carelessness and laxity are conspicuous. It *does* mean, however, that an effective routine is intelligible to anyone who has common sense and is acquainted with the business in question. If things are done in a certain way, there is usually a sound reason. If certain rules are enforced and precautions taken, they are usually necessary. If a person wishes to understand any phase of office routine, he should try to determine the reason for it. A new worker may have to follow some routines blindly until he gets a chance to think them out, but, in the long run, common sense understanding proves more valuable than automatic, unreasoned obedience. This is especially true for the secretary, from whom a large degree of initiative is often expected.

VARIATION IN METHOD

There is, of course, some variation in method from office to office. Each business has its own individual problems, and each executive his own ideas about efficiency. Nevertheless, business organizations have many general principles of operation in common. They are all part of the same economic order, and the laws of common sense hold true for all of them.

The Secretary's Work

The secretary is an important figure in a business office. She performs a variety of duties, many of them demanding independent thought and decision. Her treatment of callers and handling of business letters help to establish the tone of a firm. She is largely responsible for the smooth functioning of the executive or executives to whom she may be specially assigned. Her position is that of an important minor hub, around which the wheels of office routine revolve.

The secretary, although she must usually be a good stenographer, is much more than that. The stenographer takes dictation and transcribes it on the typewriter. She is judged by her reliability, accuracy, and speed. Her work, though essential, is decidedly limited when compared with that of the secretary.

SCOPE OF TERM

The term secretary is a flexible one. It is applied to the general clerical, stenographic assistant and receptionist of the individual executive or professional man. Such a secretary may sometimes be shared between two or more executives, performing similar services for each. In committees, institutions, clubs, and other nonbusiness organizations the term secretary is frequently applied to an important individual who performs all the actual work necessary to execute orders and decrees. This is somewhat similar to the secretary in the small office, who may be responsible for all office routine, or to the general secretary of a large office, who may have some of the duties of an office manager.

COMMON TASKS

There are certain types of work which the business office secretary will almost certainly be called upon to perform. These are: (1) opening and sorting incoming mail; (2) taking dictation; (3) transcribing shorthand or machine dictation; (4) dispatching outgoing mail; (5) filing letters and other materials; (6) making appointments; (7) handling callers and telephone calls; and (8) running errands. There are many other types of work, however, that the secretary may also be called upon to learn and execute, among them the following: (1) the arrangement, in part, of her employer's schedule; (2) reading mail and drafting replies to routine letters; (3) organizing and managing one or more filing systems and indexes; (4) reviewing and clipping articles from periodicals and newspapers; (5) interviewing callers; (6) planning itineraries; (7) ordering office supplies; (8) handling petty cash, stamps, etc.; (9) making bank deposits; (10) writing checks and paying bills: and (11) checking bank statements.

The secretary may also be responsible for holding the petty cash box and keeping the petty cash account.

THREE GUIDES

Few secretaries have to perform all these duties. Some, on the other hand, may be expected to handle these and more. One cannot list all possible duties, since each business may have special ones attached to it. The secretary attempting to master her job and improve her efficiency has three reliable guides: the instructions of her employer, her experience, and her common sense. This section is intended as an introduction to those secretarial duties which are common to many offices.

Adjusting to a New Job

When the secretary is acquainting herself with the routine of a new position, it is a good idea for her to make a list of all tasks required, with memoranda of detailed procedures involved in the more important work. Her employer has a daily schedule, which it may become her duty to arrange, and she ought to keep a similar daily schedule for herself, with reminders of future work. She should also make a list of essential telephone numbers, and of the names of individuals and firms with which her employer comes in contact. Many of these things will soon become a part of her memory, but lists are always very helpful.

Good work cannot be done in unpleasant or uncomfortable surroundings. The responsibility for such matters lies chiefly with the employer. Nevertheless, the new secretary should keep her desk neat and clean, adjust her chair to the most comfortable height, and do whatever else she can to improve her working conditions. Her employer will appreciate this, since it increases her efficiency.

The following outline of the duties of the secretary is arranged for convenience in the order in which the tasks might ordinarily occur during the day.

The Executive's Schedule

The working hours of the modern executive must be apportioned carefully if he is to discharge his duties efficiently and advance the interests of his firm. For this purpose a series of written memoranda, entered on a desk pad or file cards, is much more reliable than memory. Many secretaries are responsible for such memoranda, and all secretaries should become familiar with the system their employers use.

SCHEDULE ENTRIES

The executive's schedule contains two types of entries: (1) reminders of daily appointments and other important non-routine business; (2) "ticklers" or reminders that preparations should be made for matters that are coming up shortly, such as taxes or bills requiring payment, conferences at which a report or set of suggestions will have to be produced, or interviews necessitating special preparation. A "tickler"—so-called because it is intended to jog or "tickle" the memory—is entered on the schedule a suitable number of days before the coming event to which it refers. If it is taken care of, it is crossed off the schedule. If not, a similar entry is made for the following day, and so on until it is taken care of. Naturally reminders and ticklers are usually both entered on the same schedule, since they are closely related.

EXECUTIVE'S DESK PAD

Whether such entries are made on desk pads, index cards, or in folders depends on their number and complexity. In any case the executive almost always keeps a desk pad, frequently divided into sections for each hour of the working day, on which both he and the secretary enter his daily appointments. Such a pad is handy to use, since appointments may be entered at the moment they are made. Tickler entries may also be made on the desk pad, but are usually kept on a separate pad or set of cards.

Too often the sheets of desk pads are torn off and discarded. As these sheets are a valuable record, some form of desk pad should be used which allows the sheets to be turned under or to one side from day to day.

SECRETARY'S DESK PAD

The secretary often finds it advisable to keep a desk pad of her own, on which are entered those things that she has been delegated to do and the things of which she is to remind her employer. The competent secretary has the knack of writing entries in a form that is clear and concise. It is unnecessary, for example, to preface each entry with the phrase "Remember to . . ." But no entry should be so brief as to be puzzling when referred to again after a few hours or days.

TICKLER FILE

A tickler file consists of a set of cards, usually about thirty in number, one for each day of the month. At the end of each day, the card for that day is taken out and filed elsewhere. Before this is done, however, the entries are either crossed off or transferred to the card for the following day. At the same time a new card is added at the end of the file, thus keeping the number of cards in the file constant.

Another type of tickler file consists of a set of folders, again one for each day. Each folder contains notations of coming events and the papers, such as tax bills, inventory forms, and letters, which bear on them. This is a convenient system for the executive, permitting him to lay his hands on the pertinent documents without delay.

Handling Incoming Mail

In a small organization one person may open and sort all the mail. In a large organization mail for executives may be handled only by their secretaries. In either case, it is essential the mail be opened in such a way that there is little chance of tearing the contents or of throwing away enclosures with the envelopes. When the contents have been shaken away from the end to be opened, the envelope is slit with a paper knife. After the contents have been removed, the envelope may be cut on three sides and the interior examined to prevent the loss of enclosures, which should be clipped to the covering letter.

SORTING MAIL

An entire delivery of mail should be opened at one time. After the letters have been opened, they should be sorted according to the nature of their contents. The custom of the office will determine the precise method of sorting, just as it will decide whether the secretary is to open letters marked "personal" or "confidential." As a rule advertisements and circulars are grouped together, orders are collected into another group, and routine correspondence is placed in a category by itself. Personal mail and letters requiring special handling are separated from all other groups.

In a small office the secretary who opens the mail usually distributes it among the individuals concerned. In a large office where the secretary is serving one executive, all the mail is placed on his desk, arranged according to the order of its importance, with the most urgent business at the top. Ordinarily the circulars and advertisements, being least important, would be placed at the bottom.

Some secretaries may be required to read incoming mail carefully, underline important matters to bring them to the executive's attention, and answer routine letters.

Taking Dictation

Success in taking dictation depends primarily on a thorough knowledge of shorthand and English, but the ability of the stenographer and the person giving dictation to work together smoothly is certainly of vital importance. The stenographer—or secretary doing stenographic work—should behave in a manner that is tactful, thoughtful, courteous, and businesslike. She should sit facing the person giving dictation, her notebook supported on the desk or some other firm surface. Most businessmen do not like to dictate to a person whose attention seems to be concentrated elsewhere. Neither do they like to have their flow of thought interrupted by a person who habitually anticipates words or constantly interrupts. The competent stenographer shows an intelligent interest in the executive's words.

PREPARATION FOR DICTATION

The secretary prepares to take dictation as soon as she has finished opening and sorting the mail. Notebooks and sharpened pencils should always be kept in the same, readily accessible place, so that there will be no delay in reporting for dictation. Several pencils should be taken into the executive's office, so that the breaking of a pencil point will not cause loss of time. Filled pages in the notebook should be fastened together with a rubber band, which makes it easier to find the proper beginning page. Notes and notebooks should always be conspicuously dated, in case the executive wishes to make a quick reference to past dictation. Most offices require all stenographers to keep a file of their filled notebooks for at least one year. Even when this is not an office rule, it is a good practice, since stenographers' notebooks are a valuable record of past business transactions.

MISSED OR CONFUSED WORDS

If, when taking dictation, the stenographer misses words or finds them confused, she may call attention to the matter by repeating the last word or phrase spoken. Or she may mark uncertain portions of her notes, and ask questions about them when the piece of dictation is finished. Pauses during dictation may be utilized in adding to and completing notes, and in reading through those which have been taken. Such readings help to fix the meaning of the notes and make the task of transcription easier. If a visitor enters the room and the executive breaks off dictating, it is customary for the stenographer to leave, unless specifically requested to remain.

DATES, NUMBERS, NAMES

Special attention should be given during dictation to dates, numbers, and unfamiliar names. Since accuracy is essential, the person giving dictation should allow the stenographer time to write these out in full.

If the dictation is too rapid, it is perfectly permissible for the secretary to request a more moderate pace. Most executives prefer such requests and questions about wording rather than spoiled stationery and time wasted through enforced retyping.

Transcribing Shorthand

No system of shorthand is infallible in practice. Therefore shorthand notes cannot be transcribed automatically. Constant exercise of thought and judgment is necessary. It is a good idea to read each letter quickly before beginning to type it, in order to get a general idea of the contents. Then each sentence should be read for meaning and consistency before being typed out. This avoids erasures. It is wise to check dates and names against either enclosures or previous correspondence. Meaningless or ridiculous sentences should be questioned; otherwise retyping will obviously be necessary. Doubtful material should be questioned, or at least indicated by a lightly penciled question mark in the margin. The extent to which the stenographer may correct or improve wording depends entirely on the office and executive. In any case, she should watch out for excessive verbiage and words awkwardly repeated, since many dictators, when groping for words, tend to throw in unnecessary phrases.

TELEGRAMS

In doing transcription, immediate attention should be given to telegrams and special instructions. Such notes should be prominently marked to distinguish them from the others. Telegrams should be transcribed and sent before letters are transcribed.

The transcriber should not hesitate to consult the dictionary and other authoritative works when in doubt. It is essential that the letter be cast in a proper form and effectively arranged on the page, and that the rules of proper spelling and good English be followed. For information on the form, arrangement, style, and content of business letters, the reader is referred to chapter 3.

CARBON COPIES

Unless otherwise instructed, the transcriber should always make at least one carbon copy of each letter, usually for filing with correspondence. Sometimes additional carbon copies will be needed, especially in the case of orders and instructions. If more than four carbon copies are to be made on a manual typewriter, a hard platen should be used; otherwise the lower carbons will not be legible.

Before submitting letters for signature, the transcriber should assure herself that they make sense, and that the typing is mechanically correct. The work of a good typist differs radically from that of an amateur. In addition to speed, it shows accuracy, uniformity of impression (all the characters being struck with equal force, so that they are alike in degree of density), and a pleasing arrangement of lines and margins.

Copy Typing

It is always possible to make mistakes when transcribing shorthand notes or in interpreting the words of a person giving dictation, but in copying materials already typed or printed the secretary is expected to do a perfect job. There is no excuse for mistaking definite words and characters.

Since such copies are usually of documents, contracts, and letters received, absolute accuracy is essential. Copies should always be headed by the word "Copy" in parentheses, and any signatures should be preceded by "signed," also in parentheses. Unless the secretary is instructed otherwise, all apparent errors in the original should be copied faithfully. It is a common practice, however, to place an asterisk (*) after such errors and, at the bottom of the page, another asterisk, followed by a footnote explaining that the error occurs in the original. In the most strict variety of this work, such as that performed in legal offices, it may be necessary to copy line for line and page for page. All copy typing should be proofread against the original for errors.

Typing clean copies of rough drafts made by someone in the firm is quite a different matter, and the secretary is usually permitted to make corrections in spelling and grammar. If the meaning of some phrase cannot be determined, she should not hesitate to consult the writer.

Drafting Letters

In some offices it is part of the secretary's job to prepare replies to routine letters. She should learn to decide quickly which letters are routine and which are not. Her answers should be clearly reasoned and to the point. The general instructions contained in chapter 3 (LETTER WRITING) should be followed. According to the common procedure, she submits her replies to her employer for reading or signature at the same time that she shows him the incoming letters. This arrangement saves time.

Handling Outgoing Mail

Presuming that the letter has been typed and read, and the envelope typed, there are still certain precautions that the secretary should automatically take. She should make sure that the address on the envelope is identical with that given in the letter. She should assure herself that the letter has been signed. Finally, she should glance through the letter to ascertain what enclosures should be included, and then check the enclosures accordingly.

FOLDING

The letter should be neatly folded so that it occupies most of the envelope but leaves ample space for opening the letter without danger of tearing the contents. Small supplementary folds made at the last minute have an ugly and untidy appearance. There is no excuse for them. The secretary should determine beforehand the best way of folding the different sizes of paper used in her office. Enclosures should usually be clipped to the letter, in order to avoid being lost. If pressure must be applied in sealing an envelope, it is advisable to place a sheet of paper over the flap, in order to avoid smudges. Postage should be affixed securely, after it has been checked for correct value.

To expedite business transactions, it is important that letters be mailed promptly. The accomplished secretary knows the times at which letters are collected from the box used by her office, and plans the mailing of batches of letters accordingly. If speed is essential, letters may be sent straight to the main postoffice, and letters or packages may be sent direct to local destinations by messenger.

Detailed information on postal regulations, classes of mail, and services is contained in chapter 5.

Filing Systems

In an efficient office, all materials pertaining to business transactions are made readily available for reference by a suitable filing system. The backbone of the system is almost always a correspondence file, consisting of folders, one for each separate firm or individual with whom there are business dealings—customers, creditors, manufacturers, and advertising agencies. Each folder contains letters received from the firm in question, carbon copies of letters sent in reply, and other pertinent documents, such as advertising matter and reports on interviews and conferences. The contents of each folder are arranged in the order of their dates, and therefore tell a complete, coherent story of vital importance to a businessman wishing to review for one purpose or another the stages in a set of transactions.

The secretary may be responsible for keeping such a file in order and up to date. She should file carbon copies of the letters which she has written for her employer. She may frequently be called upon to find material in the files.

ARRANGEMENT OF ITEMS

The arrangement of items (folders, in the case of the correspondence file) is almost always alphabetical. There is a detailed discussion of this method in chapter 6. Other arrangements include the geographical, in which firms are grouped by regions, a method convenient for sales campaigns and distributions; the numerical; and the Dewey Decimal Classification, familiar in libraries. The latter method is seldom used in business offices.

Cardboard guides are used to separate the folders in a file. These guides bear identification tabs, which facilitate locating the material.

CARD INDEX

A large file is generally accompanied by a card index, in which each folder is represented by a corresponding card bearing the name of the firm or individual. If a firm is known by several different names, or different forms of the same name, there are cross reference cards; as, for example, "Corrugated Box and Fiberboard, Inc. Look under: Midwestern Corrugated Box and Fiberboard." Or "Antiquarian Society of America. See American Antiquarian Society." Similar cross reference cards would be used if the correspondence for two related firms happened to be filed in the same folder. Use of an index eliminates time wasted in long searches through the bulkier files. For a small file, however, an index is seldom worth the time necessary to maintain it.

There are many supplementary files and indexes used in business offices. These may include mailing lists, lists of customers and prospective customers, files of newspaper and magazine clippings, legal documents, receipts, orders, employee records, and indexes of references to books. In large offices each executive maintains an individual file of matters pertaining to his special province, and this file is usually kept in order by his private secretary.

MAILING LIST

A mailing list of any size is best kept on a series of cards, one for each firm or individual, rather than on typewritten sheets. Names can then be added to or dropped from the list without the need for a lengthy retyping and without disturbing the convenient alphabetical order. For similar reasons, card indexes of the names of customers and "prospects" are advisable. These may also be classified according to the item in which the customer is most interested, cards of a different color being used for this purpose; for example, a firm dealing in hardware might list purchasers of kitchen utensils on green cards, purchasers of tools on yellow cards, and general purchasers on white cards. Then if a special sales campaign for one type of product were undertaken, the appropriate cards could quickly be removed from the file.

EFFICIENT FILING

There are certain general suggestions to follow for efficient filing:

1. A file or index is only valuable if kept up to date. Otherwise it is a source of error and confusion. When a firm changes its name or address, a new card should be made out immediately, and correspondence transferred to a new folder.

2. Care should be taken to list firms according to their complete, official name.

3. If there is doubt as to where an item should most properly be filed, the quickest thing to do is to file it arbitrarily in one place and then make out a number of cross reference cards.

4. Prior to being filed, material may be kept in a general "suspense folder." However, the contents of the suspense folder should be filed as soon as possible; otherwise it will quickly become larger than the file itself. Instead of a single suspense folder, several may be used, one for each type of material, thus allowing for a certain amount of preliminary filing.

5. It is advisable to have a definite charge-out procedure, to guard against the loss of materials and to facilitate locations of materials temporarily out of the files. Out guides, out folders, and

substitution cards are the most familiar aids in charge-out systems. When materials or folders are removed from the files, one of these aids is used to replace it. On it is noted a record of by whom the material was borrowed and when. If the entire contents of a folder must be borrowed, the original folder should be kept in the file and the materials should be given to the borrower in a new, properly labeled folder. Any material received subsequent to the loan may then be filed in the original folder, eliminating the risk of misplacement of new materials before the borrowed ones are returned to the file.

6. Letters and other related papers are less bulky if stapled rather than clipped together.

7. Bulky material, such as catalogs, samples, and pamphlets, should be kept in a separate file or case, with cross reference cards indicating the location.

8. The drawers of a filing cabinet should be kept closed when not in immediate use, and locked when the office is empty.

9. The materials most frequently referred to should be kept where most easily reached, usually in the upper file drawers rather than in those next to the floor.

10. If several different folder files are in use in an office, it is well to mark the

folders constituting each file with tabs of the same color, thus preventing folders from being returned to the wrong file.

The Treatment of Callers

If a caller does not have an appointment, it is the secretary's duty to learn the nature of his business. This she does in a polite and cordial manner. Although in many cases she may have to consult with her employer, usually she must decide, on the basis of her experience, whether the caller's business is such as to require her employer's attention or might better be handled by someone else. If the business should be handled by her employer and he is busy at the time, she may arrange for a later appointment. The secretary should do her best to lighten the visitor's disappointment and send him away in a good humor if he cannot be granted an interview.

ACTING AS BUFFER

Many employers wish their secretaries to act as buffers between them and callers they are unable or unwilling to see. Secretaries in this rather uncomfortable position are required to exercise a good deal of tact and patience. A secretary who can perform such a difficult task well, and who, in addition, can transact business with routine callers without referring them to her employer at all, is a very great asset to a business.

Many offices keep a daily list of callers, each entry ordinarily including the name of the caller, his business connection, and the errand on which he called. The lists are usually filed and retained as a semipermanent record.

TELEPHONE CALLS

The handling of telephone calls is essentially the same as the handling of callers. In both cases the secretary's duty is to learn the caller's business in as brief and courteous a way as possible, and then to refer the call in the manner determined by her experience. A cheerful voice creates a good impression. If a call must be kept waiting for some time before being answered by the person to whom it is referred, it is a good idea for the secretary to make occasional reassuring remarks so that the caller will not feel he has been forgotten or slighted. It is a good practice to keep a list of telephone calls similar to the list of those who call in person.

Appointments and Itineraries

In addition to scheduling her employer's day at the office, the secretary may be required to make arrangements for his time spent outside the office—such as visits to other firms or extended trips for sales and conferences. For this purpose it is desirable that she have a good working knowledge of local transportation facilities, general traveling conditions, and her employer's personal preferences in such matters. Naturally she should consult him when in doubt, but if she performs her task sensibly and efficiently, he will come to rely greatly on her judgment.

In making appointments, courtesy and the dignity of her firm are important considerations. Where possible, appointments should be definite rather than tentative, and arranged by one phone call rather than several.

BREAKING AN APPOINTMENT

An appointment broken or delayed often results in upsetting important plans. If an appointment must be broken, notification should be given at the earliest possible moment, with an explanation. An immediate attempt should be made to set up a new appointment.

There are certain hours of the working day during which an executive can best afford to be absent from the office. Such hours, often those of the afternoon, are most suitable for outside appointments. It is often expedient to combine business and social engagements by having a meeting during luncheon.

Before leaving for his appointment, the employer will usually want to refresh his mind by going over recent notes and correspondence concerning the person he is going to meet. Therefore, the appropriate folder should be brought to his attention, with notes on plans or proposals that he may wish to discuss.

EXTENDED TRIP

Preparing an itinerary for an extended trip is a more complicated task, and usually involves the purchase of airline tickets, making hotel reservations, and making appointments in advance by letter or telephone. Very often the secretary will rely, to an extent, on the advice of a travel agent, but she must be careful to adopt an arrangement suited to her employer's preferences and convenience. It is wise for her to have timetables on hand, though great care should be taken to renew these whenever there is a change of schedules.

All arrangements should be confirmed by telephone or letter. Hotel reservations may be made by letter or through the local reservation service provided by many hotel systems, but written confirmation should always be requested. The accomplished secretary familiarizes herself with the travel and hotel facilities in those regions to which her employer's business interests are likely to carry him.

Economy of time and movement are essential points to be considered in planning itineraries. If several cities are to be visited, appointments should be made in such an order as to involve the least amount of traveling.

WRITTEN ITINERARY

After the itinerary has been arranged, it should be drawn up on paper. A brief itinerary may indicate only the hours of arrival and departure, including, of course, the name of the airline and the flight number. A more complete itinerary indicates hotel reservations, time and place of appointments, names of individuals to be met, notes on matters to be discussed, plans and suggestions, subsidiary matters to be taken up if there is time available, and local transportation arrangements. Such an itinerary is chiefly for the convenience of the traveler, but copies should always be kept at the office. Then it will be possible to get in touch with the traveler if any important instructions or periodic reports are to be forwarded to him.

The secretary may pack for the trav-

eler a special folder containing such
office supplies as blank letterhead paper, plain paper, notebooks and pencils
if there will be occasion to use them.

Care of Office Equipment

Secretaries are not usually mechanics,
and they are not expected to repair
their own typewriters. They are, however, supposed to clean and oil them in
accordance with the manufacturer's instructions. The ability of the secretary to
turn out good work depends largely on
remembering to change the ribbon of
her machine and cleaning its type whenever necessary. The care of office equipment involves covering typewriters,
adding machines, and other office machines at the end of the working day,
and dusting desks and office equipment
at regular intervals. The interior portions of typewriters may be dusted effectively with a narrow, long-handled
brush.

The secretary is often her employer's
business housekeeper. In many offices
the appearance of his desk is as much
her responsibility as is the taking of his
dictation. However, she should never
rearrange his desk without determining
whether that is agreeable to him.

Ordering Supplies

It may also be part of the secretary's duties to order office supplies. These usually include: letterheads; carbon paper; second sheets for carbon copies; envelopes, both blank and with the firm's name and address; postage; stenographic notebooks; memorandum pads; index cards; file folders; labels; tabs; bank deposit slips; pencils; pens; erasers for pencil, ink, and typewriter; clips; staples; pins; typewriter ribbons; oil for typewriter; paste; and transparent mending tape. In a large office she is more often required to requisition supplies from another department of the firm. In either case, it is her business to see that the quantities on hand are always adequate. Supplies should never be ordered in such quantities, however, that they deteriorate before use.

Bank Accounts

The handling of a bank account involves three chief operations: (1) making deposits; (2) writing checks and paying bills, (3) checking bank statements.

Checks issued and deposits made should always be entered in the stub portion of the check book, with the subtractions and additions made immediately so that the exact balance may be ascertained at a glance.

If possible, bills should be paid by check. When this is impossible, a receipt should be obtained for the cash disbursed. All offices have a procedure for verifying bills before paying them. These procedures always include verification of quantity, quality, and specifications; the checking of credit allowances and discounts; and the checking of the arithmetic of the bill.

CHECKING A BANK STATEMENT

When the bank statement and cancelled checks for the previous period are received from the bank, the secretary should go over them carefully. Checking a bank statement involves these processes:

1. The cancelled checks should be checked against the stubs in the check book and the withdrawal items on the bank statement.

2. The deposit items on the bank statement should be checked against the deposits recorded in the check book.

3. The total of deposits should be added to the balance on hand when the bank statement covering the preceding period was reconciled; from this figure the total of the checks issued during the period should be deducted. The amount then arrived at should equal the

balance shown on the bank statement and that in the check book, provided there were no deposits in transit and no outstanding checks at the date of the bank statement. Any deposits in transit should be added to, and any outstanding checks should be deducted from, the balance given on the bank statement; the result should equal the balance in the check book less any bank charges.

The Large Office

The routine of a large office has certain special characteristics setting it off from that of a small office. As a result of the difference in size, the number of tasks are multiplied. The proper execution of such a complex routine is far beyond the powers of one secretary of general ability, or even several. Specialization is essential, each employee concentrating on a few steps in a highly complicated process. Even the work of the private secretary is usually limited to that entailed in serving one executive or a small group in a specialized field.

This specialization, though inescapable, brings up certain difficulties seldom found in small offices. Greater dependence must be placed on a carefully planned routine. Yet the specialized office worker performing only one task has difficulty in understanding the function of his work and seeing it in the proper perspective, and when tasks are performed by many individuals instead of one or two, there is a correspondingly greater chance for misunderstanding, error, and confusion.

SHIFTING WORKERS

To offset this disadvantage, many large offices make a practice of shifting workers from one task to another, so that they will gain a greater understanding of the whole routine and be better able to detect errors. Some workers resent being assigned to new tasks. They dislike the added mental effort involved and think it merely a matter of whim. Actually they should welcome such opportunities and look upon them as training for promotion. This is even more true when individuals are shifted from department to department, spending a certain amount of time in production work, advertising, merchandising, sales work, and distribution. Such varied training is a frequent preliminary to advancement. The wider your knowledge, the better are your chances for promotion.

It must always be remembered that the large general office should be an adjusting mechanism between the other departments, which have a less flexible sort of work and must struggle with external factors—the production department with machines and materials, the distribution department with transportation facilities, the sales department with general business conditions and consumers' demands. Unfortunately some office administrators consider that their job is to exercise authority and direct the activities of all other departments. This mistaken authoritarianism is largely an inheritance from the days of smaller businesses, when one or a few individuals personally supervised all activities. Proper office administration coordinates activities, smooths out difficulties, avoids interdepartmental friction, and in all ways acts as an adjusting mechanism. Therefore the more flexible the individual worker is and the better he is acquainted with other jobs besides his own, the better he will be able to serve his employer and himself.

Chapter 3

LETTER WRITING

The Importance of Good Business Letters

For many secretaries, few tasks are as important or consume as much time as the writing of business letters. Some secretaries are expected merely to transcribe the letters dictated to them, with due attention to correctness and appearance; others have the additional responsibility of determining the wording of letters. Since secretaries are judged largely by the quality of their letters, they should become thoroughly familiar both with the effective use of English, and with correct business letter usage in the arrangement of parts, spelling, punctuation, and related subjects treated in this office manual.

LETTERS REFLECT COMPANY

Secretaries will sense the importance of this phase of their work when they realize that every letter reveals the character and personality of the organization which sends it. If the letter is intelligently composed and carefully typewritten, it adds to the recipient's respect for the organization, and in the long run to the esteem upon which a company's reputation and good will are based. The business letter thus has a role much like that of a firm's personal representative, who may impart either very favorable or extremely unfavorable impressions of his organization. The successful representative takes pains both to dress well and to approach his clients in a correctly trained manner. It rests with the secretary to see that the letter produces the proper effect by being suitably worded and neatly typed.

The importance of excellent business letters is increased by the permanence of the impression they produce, since all correspondence is kept on file, at least until it becomes certain that it will no longer be needed. In this way a letter may serve for a long time as a point of contact between organizations and individuals. Every time the executive reviews a file of correspondence, he experiences again the pleasant or unpleasant impressions that the letters produced when first received. Time expended in the careful preparation of letters is therefore time well invested.

EXECUTIVES' METHODS

Of course, the duties of the secretary in the writing of letters vary widely according to the individual situation. Some executives make a practice of indicating the essentials of the letter in a few general sentences, and require the secretary to express their ideas in appropriate words. The secretary should have a practical knowledge of writing methods to perform such a task successfully; and the person who has this ability is an indispensable and highly valued assistant. Other executives dictate the letter in full. Some resent the change of a word or a punctuation mark as unwarranted presumption, and expect the secretary only to typewrite the letter exactly as dictated, putting the parts in proper order and spacing the materials correctly on the page. But with either method of work the secretary who is perfectly informed in letter-writing usages will achieve the most satisfactory results.

The Language of Business Letters

Letters are of two main kinds: business letters and social letters. The letters that a secretary in a business office prepares are usually of the first kind. In social correspondence between friends a good deal of latitude is permitted in the choice of words and the arrangements of parts, but in the business letter it is necessary to follow conventional usage with greater strictness. The body of the business letter offers scope for individuality of treatment, but business letters may not use slang and the freedom of treatment that are acceptable in letters between friends. Both business and social letters require the observance of correct grammar, punctuation, and spelling at all times.

DIGNIFIED CORDIALITY

In general terms, the most effective business letters are those which combine cordiality with dignity. Such letters convey to the reader a sense of the sincerity and friendliness of the writer, and promote the objectives with which the letter is sent. Cordiality in business letters, however, degenerates into effusiveness if used to excess, sounding hollow and defeating its purpose of making the recipient wish to cooperate with the writer.

Courtesy and correctness are essential in all business correspondence, but the general tone will vary somewhat with the type of letter, depending upon whether an order for merchandise, a recommendation, a letter of information, an adjustment, or a sales letter is being written. An application for employment or a communication to an important government official is necessarily more formal and respectful than the ordinary business letter. Each sort of letter has a particular objective, and each should use the language and arrangement best suited for its attainment. Correspondence between people who have had a long business association in which an element of friendship may have entered usually is not as dignified and formal as correspondence between people who are communicating for the first time.

TRITE EXPRESSIONS

The message of the letter should be expressed in simple and natural terms. There are dozens of conventional phrases that have become so hackneyed that they have ceased to have any meaning, while others are unduly brief. Both types should be avoided entirely, since they destroy the clarity of the letter and make it seem old-fashioned. A business letter should resemble neither a telegram nor an engraved invitation to tea. Hence it should not contain telescoped expressions like "as per" and "in re," or effusions of pretended gratitude such as "your esteemed favor" and "thanking you in advance." Instead, brevity should be the result of clear thinking and the avoidance of repetition. Courtesy should be present throughout the message, rather than being injected here and there by the use of a trite phrase.

Some of the trite and objectionable phrases that should be avoided in the interest of concise and unaffected expression follow. Besides the ones listed, there are many others which the alert person will learn to detect and avoid.

ADVISE. Should not be used in the sense of *tell* or *inform*.

AFOREMENTIONED. Appropriate in legal writing, but in business correspondence *mentioned previously* or *referred to above* would be acceptable.

AS PER. A correct phrase is *according to*.

ATTACHED FIND. If it is attached, it will be found. It is better to say *attached is*.

ATTACHED HERETO. *Hereto* is superfluous.

AT YOUR CONVENIENCE; AT AN EARLY DATE. Better be more specific. It may never be convenient; what is early to your reader may be late to you.

BEG TO ACKNOWLEDGE, ADVISE, INFORM, STATE. To *beg* means to beseech or implore, or to ask for charity. None of these fits the intention of the writer. Omit the expression and simply say or do something.

CONSIDERED OPINION. Opinions customarily are reached through consideration. Omit *considered*.

CONTENTS CAREFULLY NOTED. One is expected to notice the contents of letters

SECRETARY'S/STUDENT'S GUIDE

carefully. It is a waste of time to tell the correspondent that this has been done.

DICTATED BUT NOT READ. The letter of a correspondent who uses this expression ought to be returned with the notation "Received but not read."

EAGERLY AWAIT. Not to be used unless one means to indicate either great enthusiasm or impatience.

HEREIN, HERETO, HEREWITH. All superfluous; just *enclose, attach,* or *send.*

HOPING TO HEAR FROM YOU. This is usually taken for granted.

IN DUE COURSE. This is too indefinite.

IN RE. A Latin term meaning "concerning," or "in the matter of." Should not be used except in legal writing.

KINDLY. This is an adverb meaning, generally, in a kind manner or spirit. Asking a correspondent to "Kindly fill out the enclosed form" might be presumptuous. Just say *please.*

PERMIT ME TO SAY. Since it is your letter, you need not request permission to make a comment. Omit the expression.

PLEASE BE ADVISED. Unnecessary introduction to a statement. Go right into whatever it is you intend to tell your reader.

RECENT DATE. A letter should be referred to either by the exact date or the subject, or by both.

REGRET TO STATE. Very stilted; better to say *sorry that*.

SAME. Should not be used as a pronoun except in legal documents.

THANKING YOU IN ADVANCE. It is presumptuous to assume that a request will be granted.

THE WRITER; THE UNDERSIGNED. The former is affected; the latter is appropriate in legal writing only. The pronoun *I* is correct.

THIS IS IN REPLY TO. Perfectly obvious from the contents of the letter.

TRUST YOU WILL. To be avoided unless you are quite confident. It generally is safer to say *hope you will*.

WISH TO ACKNOWLEDGE, INFORM, SAY. Just *acknowledge, inform, or say*.

Five Essentials of Business Letter English

The language used in every business letter, regardless of type, must contain five qualities that are indispensable in effective correspondence. These are:

1. Clearness
2. Conciseness
3. Completeness
4. Courtesy
5. Correctness

The writer who keeps these "Five C's" constantly in mind while composing the letter will find his task greatly simplified. Also, in reviewing the letter after it is drafted, he can estimate the value of his work according to the presence or absence of these qualities. The "Five C's" are the characteristics of good correspondence.

CLEARNESS

A letter is first of all a message to a reader. If the reader does not grasp this message easily and thoroughly, the letter has failed in its purpose, no matter how correct its form or how attractive its appearance may be. Consequently the writer must make sure that the letter conveys a message in unmistakable terms.

Clarity in letters can be achieved by following a very simple but important procedure. Before beginning the composition of the letter the writer must determine definitely what he wishes to say—whether or not he will order the materials, supply the information, give the recommendation, or do whatever else the reader has requested. If one waits until the actual writing of the letter to make these decisions, ambiguity and indecisiveness are almost certain to result. Although such a caution may appear obvious and needless, many letters are begun before the writers know what they are going to say.

After this first step, which is a matter of individual consideration for each case, the writer must find the best words for expressing the message decided upon. Clearness in the actual writing is attained by care in the selection of words; in the punctuation, the length, and arrangement of sentences; and the paragraphing. It is important to avoid vague words or those subject to misinterpretation. Sentences should be as direct as possible, not weighed down by parenthetical expressions, subordinate clauses, or participial phrases. In addition, sentences in a business letter should be reasonably brief, though too many very short sentences in succession give an undesirable staccato effect. Both vocabulary and sentence structure must be adapted to the intelligence and education of the reader. The principles of good paragraphing must also be observed, so that each topic or group of related topics occupies a paragraph by itself.

CONCISENESS

The businessman has so many claims on his limited time that he welcomes methods that conserve his working hours and energy. The best business letters, therefore, are those which enable him to grasp their message with the greatest ease and rapidity. Therefore, clearness in words and grammatical structure are necessities; another is conciseness. Conciseness in writing includes the omission of unessential matter, and the avoidance of repetition and of unduly long forms of expression. It should be noted, however, that concise writing need not be incomplete nor discourteous writing. Essential facts must not be overlooked, and the brusqueness which would result from the deletion of all expressions of cordiality and good will is undesirable.

The letter writer can find no better way to train himself in conciseness than to review his completed letters and note the number of phrases, words, and even whole sentences that could be left out without impairing the meaning of the whole.

COMPLETENESS

The completeness of the message should never be sacrificed in an exaggerated effort to achieve brevity of expression. Every item that is essential must be included in the letter, for omission of important details is likely to cause confusion. The writer's best way of avoiding this difficulty is to check over the items he intends to mention before the letter is begun, making sure that he has in mind all the necessary details and no more. The letter should be read through after it has been written, to see whether it complies with the requirements of completeness. If something has been forgotten, the letter should probably be rewritten, since details tacked on in a postscript are an admission that the letter was inexpertly drafted in the first place.

COURTESY

Every successful business organization shows great courtesy in personal contacts with individuals and other companies, for much of its success depends on the esteem of its clients and associates. Courtesy in business letters is no less essential, especially in view of the permanence of correspondence.

There is a great difference, however, between true courtesy, which consistently takes into account the problems, needs, and feelings of the reader, and sham courtesy. The latter expresses itself in resounding phrases which do not truly represent the sentiments of the writer. Furthermore, exaggerated expressions of thanks and esteem are in poor taste, even when they are sincere.

Courtesy depends in part on a properly chosen salutation and complimentary close, but to a much greater degree on the language in the body of the letter. True consideration rests in the acts of the individual or company, but whether these favor or disfavor the reader's interests, they must be communicated in courteous terms. With skill, even collection letters or refusals to grant charge accounts can be stated with a minimum of vexation to the reader. Business letters of this type should show respect for the dignity and character of the recipient, and should avoid imputing bad faith to him. Sarcasm and abuse should never appear in business letters of any kind, since they brand the writer as ill-bred, and antagonize the reader.

CORRECTNESS

Correctness in the business letter is a requirement so absolute that without it the time spent in drafting a clear, well-phrased, and courteous message is hardly worthwhile, for a letter that contains errors in formal details furnishes a sorry impression of the intelligence and character of the individual or firm that sent it. A carefully worded but carelessly transcribed letter is as ineffectual as a well-informed speaker with a severe stammer: neither the letter nor the speaker wins the favorable attention deserved by the quality of the message.

After the letter is dictated, but before it is typewritten, it should be checked for correctness in the following particulars: (1) grammar, (2) spelling, (3) capitalization, (4) punctuation, (5) the form of numerical expressions, and (6) abbreviations. When it is ascertained that the letter is correct in these usages, it should be typewritten with care, so that errors of fact do not creep in, and in accordance with the recommendations for spacing and the order of parts found in the following pages.

The Form of Business Letters

The letter's neat and pleasing appearance, like its correctness in details, enhances the value of skillful phrasing. Furthermore, clear-cut paragraph separations and proper spacing of the materials on the page permit quicker comprehension of the contents. Also, paper of good quality and a well-designed letterhead reflect credit on the writer.

A black typewriter ribbon is commonly used, although colors such as deep brown or very dark blue, to match the imprint on the letterhead, are not uncommon. Whatever the color, if the ribbon is made of cloth it should be fresh enough to provide a clear imprint. Carbon ribbons are, of course, made for single usage and therefore always produce clear, even copy. They are usable, however, only on typewriters that are made or adapted for them.

AVOIDING SMUDGES

Carelessness in making corrections may produce smudges on the page. Such smudges can be avoided by using a celluloid or plastic cutout which exposes only the letter or word to be erased. Other aids are correction fluid (painted over the error) and correction paper (which obliterates the error with a white coating when the error is retyped over a piece of correction paper placed between the ribbon and the copy). Typographical errors should not be struck over with the correct letter; instead, the error should be carefully eradicated and the proper symbol typed in its place. Since it is difficult to insert the correction in exactly the right spot after the page has been removed from the typewriter and then replaced, it is best to read the letter over for errors before taking it out of the machine.

Few business letters run longer than one page. When they do, however, the bottom of the first sheet must not be crowded. Nor should the first page be crowded to avoid using a second. The second page should be headed with the name of the addressee, the page number, and the date, thus:

Mr. Ralph C. Roberts   2.   June 30, 1976

Or, the same information may be placed

in the upper left-hand corner of the second page, as follows:

Mr. Ralph C. Roberts
June 30, 1976
Page 2

Letterhead stationery is not used for any page after the first. If specially imprinted sheets are not available (usually just the firm's name in small type), plain paper of the same stock as the letterhead should be used.

Carbon copies of all letters should be made and promptly filed. This practice makes the review of correspondence an easy matter, and is essential for a smoothly running office. Equally essential is the permanent record that carbon copies provide.

SPACING

Proper spacing of the materials on the page has a great effect on the letter's legibility and attractiveness. The letter should be approximately centered on the page, but with the upper and left-hand margins slightly wider than the lower and the right-hand margins. If the letter occupies a full page or more, the upper and left-hand margins should be not less than 1¼ inches wide, and the lower and right-hand margins not less than 1 inch wide. A shorter letter will require wider margins, but these should maintain the same proportions. The length of the lines also varies according to the length of the letter. A letter of 100 words or less presents the best appearance if the lines are about 40 characters long (counting both letters and the spaces between words). A letter containing from 100 to 150 words should have 50-character lines; one of more than 150 words should have 60-character lines. If the typewriter used has "elite" type (that is, type which measures 12 characters to the inch), letters exceeding 200 words in length should have 70-character lines; but if the typewriter has larger type than this, a line of 70 characters will be too long for the minimum margins of $1\frac{1}{4}$ inch and 1 inch. Before the transcription of the letter is begun the typist should make an approximate estimate of its length and set the typewriter's margin guides accordingly.

The length of the letter determines not only the preferable width of the lines, but also the vertical spacing. If the letter is a very brief one, it is likely to appear lost in a sea of white paper. This may be avoided by increasing the number of blank lines between the various parts of the letter, in order to expand it vertically on the page. The area which the letter covers on the page may also be increased by double-spacing.

LAYOUT

The most commonly used styles of layout are block, full-block, and semi-block. The simplified style is also frequently used, while the once popular indented style is now rarely seen. Punctuation styles, too, have changed. The formerly common closed punctuation required suitable marks after the date line, each line of the address, the salutation, the complimentary close, and each line of the signature. At the opposite extreme is open punctuation, which eliminates all marks unless a line happens to end in an abbreviation. Standard punctuation, the most generally used form, calls only for a colon after the salutation and a comma after the complimentary close (plus, of course, a period when a line ends in an abbreviation).

BLOCK STYLE

The inside address, the attention line, the salutation, the identification line, and the paragraphs begin flush with the left-hand margin; the date ends flush with the right-hand margin or is centered under the letterhead imprint; and the complimentary close and signature lines begin slightly to the right of center. Standard or open punctuation may be used, but standard is the more common.

FULL BLOCK STYLE

All components begin at the left-hand margin. Standard or open punctuation may be used. The dictator's initials are not included in the identification line.

SEMI-BLOCK STYLE

The same as block style, except that the paragraphs are indented five or ten spaces, or to the colon after a short salutation. Standard punctuation is usual.

SIMPLIFIED STYLE

The same as full-block style but with no salutation or complimentary close. Usually a subject line (concocted if necessary) is placed between the address and the body of the letter. Open punctuation is used, and the dictator's initials are not included in the identification line.

The Parts of Business Letters

The business letter consists of seven main parts, found in the following order: (1) heading, (2) date, (3) address, (4) salutation, (5) body, (6) complimentary close, and (7) signature.

HEADING

The heading consists of the name and address of the sender, imprinted or engraved at the top of the sheet. The term *letterhead* applies to the heading as well as to the imprinted sheet as a whole.

DATE

Placement of the date varies according to the style of layout used, as explained in the preceding section. Neither abbreviations nor figures should be used for the month; nor should "st," "nd," "rd," or "th" follow the day of the month. The year should not be represented by an apostrophe followed by two digits. Correct and incorrect forms of the date line are illustrated below:

INCORRECT

Nov. 23, 1977

CORRECT

November 23, 1977

INCORRECT

12/11/77

CORRECT

December 11, 1977

INCORRECT

January 6th, 1977

CORRECT

January 6, 1977

INCORRECT

April 17, '77

CORRECT

April 17, 1977

ADDRESS

The address in the letter follows the same form as that on the envelope. It should contain the name, street address, city, state, and zip code of the addressee. The name of a well-known office building sometimes supplements or replaces the street address. If a company name appears in the address, it should be the full, official name.

When a letter is addressed to an individual within a company, the business title always follows the name, on the same line or, if it is a long title, on the line below. The title should never be abbreviated. The only words that precede the name of an individual are courtesy titles ("Mr.," "Mrs.," "Ms.," and "Miss") and titles showing professional standing, like "Dr.," "Professor," and "The Reverend." These titles should always be used, even when a business or official title follows the name. But when initials indicating a degree follow the name, no title precedes it. Exceptions to these practices occur in addressing people of high office, as listed in chapter 4.

The following examples illustrate correct and incorrect forms for the name line of the address:

INCORRECT
Treasurer Richard J. Wilts

CORRECT
   Mr. Richard J. Wilts, Treasurer

INCORRECT
   Dr. Harold Coombs, M.D.

CORRECT
   Dr. Harold Coombs
          or
   Harold Coombs, M.D.

INCORRECT
   Professor Samuel Slaughter,
   Ph.D.

CORRECT
   Professor Samuel Slaughter
          or
   Samuel Slaughter, Ph.D.

   The address is usually placed two or
more lines below the date line, but in
government correspondence and some
very formal letters it is frequently found
below the signature, at the lower left-
hand corner of the page.
   A variety of correct complete addresses follows:

   Mr. John J. Creighton, President
   Acme Machining Company, Inc.
   630 Fifth Avenue
   New York, New York 10020

Mr. Albert M. Browning
Executive Vice President
Pacific Coast Furniture Enterprises
209 Post Street
San Francisco, California 94108

Dr. William J. Moore
Winous-Point Building
1250 Euclid Avenue
Cleveland, Ohio 44115

Charles F. Morton, Ph.D.
Institute of Geological Studies
1201 Portland Place
Boulder, Colorado 80302

Miss Rosemary Bellingham
Assistant to the President
Plymouth Electric Industries, Inc.
1168 Commonwealth Avenue
Boston, Massachusetts 02134

The Reverend Ralph C. Roberts
Executive Director
Universal Gospel Society
2611 West End Avenue
Nashville, Tennessee 37203

Mrs. George C. Hambleton
309 South Fremont Street
Tampa, Florida 33606

Joseph C. Embry, D.D.S.
2855 Sky Harbor Boulevard
Phoenix, Arizona 85034

SALUTATION

The salutation marks the formal opening of the letter. It begins at the left-hand margin, usually two spaces below the inside address. In standard punctuation it is followed by a colon. Users of the open punctuation system use no punctuation mark after the salutation.

The choice of the salutation depends on the relationship between the writer and the reader of the letter. In ordinary business correspondence, moderately dignified salutations are desirable, unless the relationship has developed into a warmly personal one, when considerable informality is permissible. Special forms of address are used in writing to government officials; these are listed in chapter 4.

The salutations suitable for various situations are as follows:

For addressing a company or a
group of men:

Gentlemen: (formal or informal)

For addressing a group of women:

Ladies: (formal or informal)
Mesdames: (formal)

For addressing an individual:

My dear Mr. O'Hara: (formal)
My dear Miss Foster: (formal)
Dear Sir: (moderately formal)
Dear Madam: (moderately
    formal)
Dear Mr. O'Hara: (moderately
    informal)
Dear Miss Foster: (moderately
    informal)

For addressing a close business
    acquaintance:

Dear Tom: (very informal)

The word "dear" in a salutation is
capitalized only if it is the first word in
the phrase. The only abbreviations used
in salutations are "Mr.," "Mrs.," "Ms.,"
"Messrs.," "Mmes.," and "Dr."
A letter addressed directly to an organization should use the salutation "Gentlemen." However, if the writer wishes
the letter to receive the attention of a
particular individual in the firm, this is
accomplished by inserting the phrase
"Attention: Mr. _____" between the last

line of the address and the salutation. In this event, either "Gentlemen" or "Dear Mr. _____" would be an acceptable salutation. The layout would be as follows:

Simmons and Tate, Inc.
20 East 82nd Street
New York, New York 10028

Attention: Mr. John W. Harris

Gentlemen: (*or* Dear Mr. Harris:)

BODY

The body of the letter is the portion that contains the message. It begins two lines below the salutation. Unless the letter is very brief, it should be single-spaced, with a double space between paragraphs. If double-spacing is used, the paragraphs must be indented. Regardless of whether standard or open punctuation is used in the other parts of the letter, the body must be punctuated in accordance with conventional usage.

Following are four examples of the different ways the body of the letter may be spaced on the letterhead:

Double-spaced indented paragraphs with no blank lines between them:

_____

_____

_____

_____

_____

_____

Double-spaced indented paragraphs
with blank line between them:

_____

_____

_____

_____

_____

_____

Single-spaced indented paragraphs
with blank line between them:

———————————————————
———————————————————
———————————————————
———————————

————————————
———————————————————
————————————————————

Single-spaced paragraphs in block style, with blank line between them:

———————————————————
———————————————————
———————————————————
———————————————————

———————————————————
———————————————————
———————————————————

If the body of the letter contains an address for the information of the reader, it is helpful to make this stand out prominently for convenience in reference. This may be accomplished by centering it on the page, as in this example:

For additional details we advise you to communicate with America's foremost authority in this field:

Dr. Franz A. Heiden
Hamm Building
St. Paul, Minnesota 55102

We feel confident that he will be glad to furnish the information you require.

COMPLIMENTARY CLOSE

The complimentary close is a formal expression of regard with which the writer takes leave of the reader. It follows the body of the letter, occupying a line by itself, two or more lines below the last line of the body. In the block and semi-block styles of layout, the complimentary close begins slightly to the right of center, while in the full-block and simplified styles it is placed flush with the left-hand margin.

The use of a particular phrase for the complimentary close, like the salutation, depends on the relationship between the sender and the receiver. The complimentary close should be consistent with the salutation in the degree of its formality.

The most frequently used complimentary closes for business correspondence are as follows:

Respectfully yours, (very formal, and used principally for government officials and people in superior positions)

Very truly yours, (moderately formal)
Yours very truly, (moderately formal)
Yours truly, (moderately formal)
Sincerely yours, (informal)
Cordially yours, (informal; most used in business correspondence between persons who know each other well)

The complimentary close should have only its first letter capitalized, and should contain no abbreviations. It should not be attached to the preceding sentence or follow such stereotyped expressions as "Hoping for a prompt reply I am . . ." It is usually followed by a comma, except when open punctuation is used.

SIGNATURE

The signature is typewritten beneath the space allowed for the handwritten signature, three or four lines below the complimentary close, depending upon the need for compressing or expanding the materials on the page. It should contain the name of the writer and his position, which may be typed on one line or two. If this information is imprinted on the letterhead, no typewritten signature is necessary.

Business titles and degree or professional letters follow the typewritten signature. Neither the handwritten nor the typewritten portions of the signature should contain personal titles, such as "Mr.," "Rev.," "Dr.," or "Professor." The only exception to this rule is the use in parentheses of "Miss" or "Mrs." when a woman chooses to so identify herself.

Illustrations of typewritten signatures follow:

Russell J. Blair, Registrar

Mary J. Valentine, Ph.D.

Charles B. Harrison, Manager
Advertising Department

John C. Worth, C.P.A.

(Mrs.) Alice C. White, Secretary

ADDITIONAL PARTS

Although they do not appear in all business letters, three additional letter parts that require attention are the identification letters, the notice of enclosure, and the postscript.

Identification Letters. The identification letters are the initials of the writer of the letter and those of the secretary who transcribed it. The initials of the writer always come first. Identification letters are placed at the left margin, a few lines below the last line of the signature, in any of the following forms:

RJMcM/EMP
RJMcM:EMP
JMcM:emp
JMcM/emp

NOTICE OF ENCLOSURE

The notice of enclosure reminds the reader that something has been enclosed with the letter. The word "Enclosure" or the abbreviation "Enc." is written just below the identification letters. If there is more than one enclosure, the number should be stated, and if the enclosure is of special importance it should be identified, as:

RJMcM/emp
Enclosures (3)

RJMcM:emp
Enc. Check, $3,024.50

POSTCRIPT

Postscripts usually are avoided, since their use may be taken as evidence of confused thinking on the part of the writer who only remembered to include an essential detail after the letter was typewritten. There are times, however, when they are deliberately used, to create emphasis. When there is a postscript it should be placed at least two lines below the identification letters, or notice of enclosure if there is one, preceded by the letters "P.S."

ENVELOPE

The envelope should be carefully typed and well-spaced. Both the sender's and the receiver's addresses should appear on the face. The address to which the letter is being sent should begin slightly more than halfway down the envelope and slightly to the left of the center. It should, of course, be identical to the address used in the letter.

The zip code should be the last notation of any kind on the envelope, to ensure expeditious handling in the mails. Should anything appear after the line on which the zip code is written, the automatic sorting machine will reject the piece of mail, throwing it aside for later manual handling. For this reason, the attention line should be placed just above and to the left of the address. The same positioning applies to notations regarding handling of the mail after it has reached its destination, such as "Personal," "Hold for Arrival," and "Please Forward." Notations concerning type of postal service (special delivery, air mail, registered mail) should be typed above and to the right of the address, directly below the place at which the postage will be affixed.

SKELETON ENVELOPE FORM

```
 _____   (Printed
 _____   Return
 _____   Address)

                              (Type of Postal Service)
                              _____

 (Attention Line)
 _____




                    _____
                    _____
                    _____
                    _____
```

SKELETON BUSINESS LETTER FORM
(Block style, standard punctuation)

Dateline
Address

Salutation

Body

Complimentary Close

Signature

Identification Initials
Enclosure Note

SKELETON BUSINESS LETTER FORM
(Full-block style, open punctuation)

Dateline

Address

Salutation

Body

Complimentary Close

Signature

Typist's Initials

Enclosure Note

SKELETON BUSINESS LETTER FORM
(Semi-block style, standard punctuation)

Dateline

Address

Salutation

Body

Complimentary Close

Signature

Identification Initials
Enclosure Note

SKELETON BUSINESS LETTER FORM
(Simplified Style)

Dateline

Address

Subject Line

Body

Signature

Typist's Initials
Enclosure Note

Chapter 4

FORMS OF ADDRESS FOR GOVERNMENT AND ECCLESIASTICAL OFFICIALS

Letters addressed to people in high positions in governmental or religious organizations require the use of special forms for the address, the salutation, and the complimentary close. Various expressions with differing degrees of formality are possible in some cases, those listed hereafter being the most formal.

The inside address in a letter to a government official may be placed either before the salutation, as in most business letters, or in the lower left-hand corner of the page below the level of the signature.

Two terms which should be used with special care are "the Honorable" and "the Reverend." Since they are adjectives rather than titles, they must be followed by the first name, the initials, or the appropriate title, rather than by the surname alone. They are usually abbreviated to "Hon." and "Rev." if the word "the" is omitted. Examples:

> The Honorable Henry Robinson
> The Honorable H. F. Robinson
> The Honorable Mr. Robinson
> *not*
> The Honorable Robinson

> Hon. H. F. Robinson
> *not*
> Hon. Robinson

> The Reverend Matthew Watts
> The Reverend M. Z. Watts
> The Reverend Dr. Watts
> *not*
> The Reverend Watts

> Rev. Matthew Watts
> *not*
> Rev. Watts

When a clergyman holds a doctoral degree, the initials of the degree should follow a comma after his name on the address line, or he may be addressed as "Rev. Dr. John F. Smith," with no initials after his name. The title "Doctor" may then be used in the salutation.

In closing a formal letter to a high governmental or ecclesiastical official, the most formally correct form for the complimentary close is "Respectfully yours," while "Very truly yours," is appropriately formal for a person of lower rank. The most common informal complimentary close is "Sincerely yours."

United States Officials

THE PRESIDENT

Address:

The President
The White House
Washington, D.C.   20500
or
The President of the United States
The White House
Washington, D.C.   20500

Salutation:

Mr. President:
or
My dear Mr. President:

Complimentary Close:

Respectfully yours,

THE VICE PRESIDENT

Address:

The Vice President
The United States Senate
Washington, D.C.   20510
or
The Honorable (FULL NAME)
Vice President of the United States
Washington, D.C.

Salutation:

Mr. Vice President:
> *or*

My dear Mr. Vice President:
Complimentary Close:
Respectfully yours,

CABINET MEMBERS

Address:
The Honorable (FULL NAME)
Secretary of (DEPARTMENT)
Washington, D.C.
Salutation:
Sir:
> *or*

My dear Mr. Secretary:
Complimentary Close:
Very truly yours,

ASSISTANT CABINET MEMBERS

Address:
The Honorable (FULL NAME)
Assistant Secretary of (DEPART-
MENT)
Washington, D.C.
Salutation:
Sir:
> *or*

My dear Mr. (SURNAME):
Complimentary Close:
Very truly yours,

CHIEF JUSTICE OF THE SUPREME COURT

Address:
The Chief Justice

The Supreme Court
Washington, D.C.   20543
Salutation:
Sir:
or
My dear Mr. Chief Justice:
Complimentary Close:
Very truly yours,

ASSOCIATE JUSTICE OF THE SUPREME COURT

Address:
Mr. Justice (SURNAME)
The Supreme Court
Washington, D.C.   20543
Salutation:
My dear Mr. Justice:
or
Dear Justice (SURNAME):
Complimentary Close:
Very truly yours,

UNITED STATES SENATOR

Address:
The Honorable (FULL NAME)
United States Senate
Washington, D.C.   20510
Salutation:
Dear Sir:
or
My dear Senator (SURNAME):
Complimentary Close:
Very truly yours,

UNITED STATES CONGRESSMAN

Address:

The Honorable (FULL NAME)
House of Representatives
Washington, D.C.   20515

Salutation:

Dear Sir:

or

My dear Mr. (SURNAME):

Complimentary Close:

Very truly yours,

State and Local Government Officials

GOVERNOR OF A STATE

Address:

The Honorable (FULL NAME)
Governor of (STATE)
(State Capitol, State)

Salutation:

Dear Sir:

or

My dear Governor (SURNAME):

Complimentary Close:

Respectfully yours,

or

Very truly yours,

STATE SENATOR

Address:

The Honorable (FULL NAME)

The State Senate
(State Capitol, State)
Salutation:
　Dear Sir:
　　　or
　My dear Senator (SURNAME):
Complimentary Close:
　Very truly yours,

STATE ASSEMBLYMAN (OR REPRESENTA-
TIVE)

Address:
　The Honorable (FULL NAME)
　Member of the Assembly
　(*or,* House of Representatives)
　(State Capitol, State)
Salutation:
　Dear Sir:
　　　or
　My dear Mr. (SURNAME):
Complimentary Close:
　Very truly yours,

MAYOR

Address:
　The Honorable (FULL NAME)
　Mayor of (CITY)
　(City, State)
Salutation:
　My dear Mr. Mayor:
　　　or
　My dear Mayor (SURNAME):
Complimentary Close:
　Very truly yours,

Diplomatic Officials

UNITED STATES AMBASSADOR

Address:

The Honorable (FULL NAME)

American Ambassador

(City and Country where stationed)

Salutation:

Sir:

or

My dear Mr. Ambassador:

Complimentary Close:

Very truly yours,

UNITED STATES CONSUL

Address:

(FULL NAME), Esquire

American Consul at (LOCATION)

(City and Country where stationed)

Salutation:

Dear Sir:

or

My dear Mr. (SURNAME):

Complimentary Close:

Very truly yours,

Roman Catholic Church Officials

POPE

Address:

His Holiness Pope (NAME)

Vatican City
Rome, Italy
Salutation:
Most Holy Father:
or
Your Holiness:
Complimentary Close:
Respectfully yours,

CARDINAL

Address:
His Eminence (GIVEN NAME) Cardi-
nal (SURNAME)
Salutation:
Your Eminence:
Complimentary Close:
Respectfully yours,

ARCHBISHOP

Address:
The Most Reverend (FULL NAME)
Archbishop of (LOCATION)
Salutation:
Your Excellency:
Complimentary Close:
Respectfully yours,

BISHOP

Address:
The Most Reverend (FULL NAME)
Bishop of (LOCATION)
Salutation:
Your Excellency:
Complimentary Close:
Respectfully yours,

PROTONOTARIES APOSTOLIC, DOMESTIC
PRELATES, AND VICARS GENERAL
    Address:
        Right Reverend Monsignor (FULL
            NAME)
    Salutation:
        Right Reverend Monsignor:
    Complimentary Close:
        Respectfully yours,

PAPAL CHAMBERLAINS
    Address:
        Very Reverend Monsignor (FULL
            NAME)
    Salutation:
        Very Reverend Monsignor:
    Complimentary Close:
        Respectfully yours,

PRIEST
    Address:
        Reverend (FULL NAME) (followed by
            letters designating his order,
            if any)
    Salutation:
        Dear Father (SURNAME):
    Complimentary Close:
        Very truly yours,

Protestant and Jewish Ecclesiastical Officials

PROTESTANT EPISCOPAL BISHOP
    Address:

The Right Reverend (FULL NAME)
Bishop of (LOCATION)
Salutation:
Right Reverend:
   or
Dear Sir:
Complimentary Close:
Respectfully yours,

PROTESTANT CLERGYMAN

Address:
The Reverend (FULL NAME) (followed by initials of degree, if any)
   or, if a Doctor of Divinity,
The Reverend Doctor (FULL NAME)
Salutation:
Reverend Sir:
   or
Dear Doctor (SURNAME):
Complimentary Close:
Very truly yours,

RABBI

Address:
Rabbi (FULL NAME)
Salutation:
Reverend Sir:
   or
Dear Rabbi (SURNAME):
Complimentary Close:
Very truly yours,

Chapter 5

POST OFFICE INFORMATION

Intelligent and economical use of the United States mails requires that the proficient secretary have a good working knowledge of the official classification system and rate structure. To avoid unnecessary delays and losses, the following recommendations should be kept in mind:

1. Be sure to give the name and address in full, with street and number, post office box, or R.F.D. address.

2. Always include zip code numbers, placing them at the end of the city and state line, two spaces after the name of the state.

3. If the name of the state must be abbreviated, use the official Post Office two-letter abbreviation (*see page 112*).

4. "General Delivery" should be written above the address on matter for persons not permanently located in the city addressed.

5. Be certain that all letters are properly sealed, and all parcels securely wrapped.

6. Make sure that address labels and postage are firmly affixed.

7. Show a return address on envelopes and packages.

Classes of Mail

A general description of the four classes of mail follows. In unusual situations or when there is doubt, specific information should be obtained from a post office.

FIRST CLASS

This classification includes post and postal cards; all matter wholly or partially in writing, whether handwritten or typewritten, sealed or unsealed; matter specifically labeled as closed against postal inspection, as explained in the descriptions of third- and fourth-class mail; and bills and statements of accounts, except invoices accompanying third-or fourth-class mail.

SECOND CLASS

Newspapers, periodicals, publications issued by and in the interests of certain nonprofit organizations and associations, classroom publications, and certain agricultural science publications are considered second-class mail.

THIRD CLASS

Third-class mail consists of matter weighing less than sixteen ounces not mailed or required to be mailed as first-class and not permissible as second-class mail. It includes circulars, books, catalogs and other printed matter, merchandise, seeds, bulbs, and plants. An invoice may be sent with the package. Sealed pieces mailed at the single-piece rate must be marked "Third Class"; there are special provisions for marking bulk third-class mail.

Mailing of sealed articles at third-class rates of postage implies the sender's consent to postal inspection of the contents. If the sender does not wish the package to be opened for inspection, it should be plainly marked "First Class" and sent at that rate of postage.

FOURTH CLASS (PARCEL POST)

Merchandise, printed matter, mailable live animals, and all other matter not considered first-, second-, or third-class mail may be sent by parcel post. The weight and size limits vary, depending upon the contents and upon the class of the post office at or to which they are mailed. An invoice may be enclosed.

There are special fourth-class rates of postage for:

1. catalogues;
2. books, 16mm or narrower film, printed music, printed objective test materials, sound recordings, and numerous other items; the address side of each such package must be marked in a manner that identifies its contents, as "Special Fourth-Class Rate—Books," or "Special Fourth-Class Rate—16mm or Narrower Film";
3. certain articles mailed by a school, college, university, public library, or nonprofit organization; the address side of each such package must bear the statement "Library Rate."

Mailing of sealed packages at fourth-class rates of postage implies the sender's consent to postal inspection of the contents. If the sender does not wish the package to be opened for inspection, it should be plainly marked "First Class" and sent at that rate of postage.

Special Types of Service

Air Mail

Any matter that is accepted for surface mail may be sent by air mail, provided it is not subject to damage or harm by changes in temperature or atmospheric pressures. It is carried by air and by the fastest connecting surface carriers. Postage is charged by weight and also, in the case of items weighing more than seven ounces, by zone, regardless of the class of mail.

SPECIAL DELIVERY

This type of service provides immediate delivery at the office of address during reasonable hours. Special-delivery mail is handled and transported in the same manner as first-class mail, regardless of the class of mail. The fee for special delivery must be prepaid in addition to the regular postage for the class of mail used.

SPECIAL HANDLING

This service is available only for third- and fourth-class mail. It offers the most expedient handling, dispatch, and transportation but does not include special delivery.

INSURANCE

Third- and fourth-class mail may be insured against loss or damage by payment of a fee in addition to the regular postage, provided the articles are sufficiently well-packaged to withstand handling in the mail.

REGISTERED MAIL

This service provides evidence of mailing and added protection for valuable and important mail as well as—with payment of an additional fee—evidence of delivery and restricted delivery (to the addressee in person). It is available for matter with postage prepaid at regular first-class or air-mail rates. Registered mail is the proper type of service to use when mailing negotiable and nonnegotiable instruments: money, valuable papers, jewelry, and other articles of unusual value. The basic fee for registry varies according to the full value of the contents, which must be declared when the matter is presented at the post office for registration.

CERTIFIED MAIL

This service also is available for matter with postage prepaid at the regular first-class or air-mail rates. Certified mail is handled in the ordinary channels, and no indemnity is provided. The service is intended for matter of no intrinsic value on which a receipt for the sender and record of delivery at the office of address is desired. Evidence of delivery and restricted delivery are available upon payment of the respective required fees. The basic fee for certified mail is a fixed charge, less than the minimum fee for registered mail.

C.O.D.

Collect-on-delivery service is provided for those who wish the price of an article to be collected from the addressee, with the amount collected remitted to the sender by the Post Office. The fee, which includes insurance against loss or damage to the article, is based upon the amount to be collected, and is in addition to regular postage. Both the fee and the postage must be prepaid, but the mailer may include these charges in the amount to be collected from the addressee.

INTERNATIONAL MAIL

There are two general categories of international mail: postal union mail and parcel post. Because of the wide variations in requirements regarding size, weight, sealing or not sealing, customs forms, and preparation for mailing, details should be obtained from a post office. A brief description of the two categories follows.

POSTAL UNION MAIL—This is divided into two groups, LC mail and AO mail. Letters, letter packages, air letters and post cards are considered LC mail. AO mail includes printed matter, samples of merchandise, matter for the blind, and small packets. Both groups may be sent by air or surface mail, at postage rates that vary according to the country of destination. Registration, return receipt, and special-delivery services are available to many countries.

PARCEL POST—Included in this category are all items that do not fit into one of the groups of postal union mail. Both air and surface parcel post are available to many countries, as is insurance, but registration is limited to only a few countries.

OFFICIAL POST OFFICE
ABBREVIATIONS

Alabama . . . . AL
Alaska . . . . AK
Arizona . . . . AZ
Arkansas . . . . AR
California . . . . CA
Colorado . . . . CO
Connecticut . . . . CT
Delaware . . . . DE
District of Columbia . . . . DC
Florida . . . . FL
Georgia . . . . GA
Guam . . . . GU
Hawaii . . . . HI
Idaho . . . . ID
Illinois IL
Indiana . . . . IN
Iowa . . . . IA
Kansas . . . . KS
Kentucky . . . . KY
Louisiana . . . . LA
Maine . . . . ME

Maryland	MD
Massachusetts	MA
Michigan	MI
Minnesota	MN
Mississippi	MS
Missouri	MO
Montana	MT
Nebraska	NE
Nevada	NV
New Hampshire	NH
New Jersey	NJ
New Mexico	NM
New York	NY
North Carolina	NC
North Dakota	ND
Ohio	OH
Oklahoma	OK
Oregon	OR
Pennsylvania	PA
Puerto Rico	PR
Rhode Island	RI
South Carolina	SC
South Dakota	SD
Tennessee	TN
Texas	TX
Utah	UT
Vermont	VT
Virginia	VA
Virgin Islands	VI
Washington	WA
West Virginia	WV
Wisconsin	WI
Wyoming	WY

Chapter 6

FILING BY ALPHABET

Alphabetizing is the basis of the filing systems used in most business offices. Although the systems in ordinary use differ in details, all are based upon the same general rules. These rules are given below. It is important to remember that occasionally offices have developed systems which depart from standard practice in some respects.

Alphabetical Arrangement

Arrange words or proper names according to the order of their first, second, third letters, carrying the process far enough to place the words in correct alphabetical order. For example:

Not Alphabetically Arranged	Alphabetically Arranged
Smithers	Smith
Smythe	Smithers
Smith	Smythe

NOT ALPHABETICALLY ARRANGED	ALPHABETICALLY ARRANGED
Abrams	Abarbanell
Abrahams	Abrahams
Abarbanell	Abrams
Bankhead	Bangs
Bangs	Bankhead
Davisson	Davidson
Davidson	Davisson
Slotkowsky	Schmidt
Slotkowski	Schultz
Schultz	Schulze
Schulze	Slotkowski
Schmidt	Slotkowsky
Winters	Stone
Witherspoon	Wallace
Wallace	Winters
Stone	Witherspoon

File the names of persons according to (1) surname, (2) given name or first initial, (3) middle name or middle initial. Initials are always filed before names beginning with the same letter. For example:

NOT ALPHABETICALLY
ARRANGED
Edward H. Bangs
E. H. Bangs
Edward Howard Bangs

Ernest H. Bangs
E. Henry Bangs
Edward Henry Bangs

ALPHABETICALLY
  ARRANGED
Bangs, E. H.
Bangs, E. Henry
Bangs, Edward H.
Bangs, Edward Henry
Bangs, Edward Howard
Bangs, Ernest H.

When names are pronounced similarly but spelled differently, enter each in the file and make a cross reference to its alternatives:

Miller; *see also* Mueller, Muller.
Mueller; *see also* Miller, Muller.
Muller; *see also* Miller, Mueller.

Prefixes, with or without capital letters, such as *de, Mac, Mc, O', van,* or *von* are treated as the first syllable of the surname, and apostrophes are disregarded:

NOT ALPHABETICALLY
  ARRANGED
Robert LaChance
Alfred von Tirpitz
Jan van Rebeck
John O'Hara
Charles MacArthur

Raoul D'Artagnan
Lee De Forest
John De Grey
Alexander de Seversky

ALPHABETICALLY
  ARRANGED
D'Artagnan, Raoul
De Forest, Lee
De Grey, John
de Seversky, Alexander
LaChance, Robert
MacArthur, Charles
O'Hara, John
van Rebeck, Jan
von Tirpitz, Alfred

Classify compound or hyphenated names by the first part of the compound:

NOT ALPHABETICALLY
  ARRANGED
Michael Forbes-Robertson
Ernestine Schumann-Heink
Stephen Byng-Enfield
Nikolai Rimsky-Korsakov

ALPHABETICALLY
  ARRANGED
Byng-Enfield, Stephen
Forbes-Robertson, Michael
Rimsky-Korsakov, Nikolai
Schumann-Heink, Ernestine

Titles, degrees, and abbreviated designations are placed last, in parentheses, and are not considered in alphabetizing except for arranging identical names:

NOT ALPHABETICALLY
    ARRANGED
Col. John Quincy Jefferson
Rev. Edward Holmes
Lady Nancy Astor
John W. Smith, Jr.
Prof. Anthony Edwards
C. Arnold McGuire, Ph.D.
John W. Smith, Sr.
Baron Nils Nordenskjold
John B. Murphy, M.D.

ALPHABETICALLY
    ARRANGED
Astor, Nancy (Lady)
Edwards, Anthony (Prof.)
Holmes, Edward (Rev.)
Jefferson, John Quincy (Col.)
McGuire, C. Arnold (Ph.D.)
Murphy, John B. (M.D.)
Nordenskjold, Nils (Baron)
Smith, John W. (Jr.)
Smith, John W. (Sr.)

When the title of nobility differs from the person's name, it is usually necessary to cross-refer to a listing by titles:

Buchan, John; *see* Tweedsmuir, Baron.

Disraeli, Benjamin; *see* Beaconsfield, Earl of.

Wellesley, Arthur; *see* Wellington, Duke of.

Names of Organizations

In general, the names of businesses, societies, and other organizations are alphabetized as printed. Be sure the correct, full name is used. There are many exceptions to the rule for institutional names, the most important of which are given below. If confusion is likely to arise, cross references should be used:

NOT ALPHABETICALLY
   ARRANGED
General Cigar Company, Inc.
Ingersoll-Rand Company
American Can Company
North American Van Lines, Inc.
Crown Zellerbach Corporation
TRW, Inc.
Swift and Company
Merck & Co., Inc.
Northwest Airlines, Inc.

ALPHABETICALLY
   ARRANGED
American Can Company
Crown Zellerbach Corporation

General Cigar Company, Inc.
Ingersoll-Rand Company
Merck & Co., Inc.
North American Van Lines, Inc.
Northwest Airlines, Inc.
Swift and Company
TRW, Inc.

An ampersand (the symbol "&"), when correctly a part of the name, should not be written out. *Brown & Jones* should not be written as *Brown and Jones.*

When *and* is spelled out in the name, the ampersand should not be used. *Jones and Brown* should not be written as *Jones & Brown.*

When the name of an institution contains the name of an individual, the individual's name determines the alphabetical classification for filing purposes:

NOT ALPHABETICALLY
  ARRANGED
A. O. Smith Corporation
Arthur G. McKee & Co.
B. F. Goodrich Company
George E. Davies Foundation
J. C. Penney Company, Inc.

ALPHABETICALLY
  ARRANGED
Davies, George E., Foundation
Goodrich, B. F., Company

McKee, Arthur G., & Co.
Penney, J. C., Company, Inc.
Smith, A. O., Corporation

The, when it occurs at the beginning of a corporate or institutional name, is placed in parentheses at the end of the name. *The Procter & Gamble Company* should be classified as *Procter & Gamble Company (The).*

Articles ("a," "an," and "the"), prepositions ("for," "in," "of," etc.), and the word "and" or the ampersand "&" within the name are disregarded in filing.

Compounds, whether formed of the names of persons or otherwise, are treated as one word:

NOT ALPHABETICALLY
  ARRANGED
Smart and Daniels
While-U-Wait Pressers
Eat-and-Drink, Inc.
Whitman and Kane
Adams-Millis Corporation
The Dow Chemical Company
Smart-Cut Clothiers, Inc.

ALPHABETICALLY
  ARRANGED
Adams-Millis Corporation
Dow Chemical Company (The)
Eat-and-Drink, Inc.
Smart-Cut Clothiers, Inc.

Smart and Daniels
While-U-Wait Pressers
Whitman and Kane

Names containing words ending in "s," with or without an apostrophe, are alphabetized as written:

NOT ALPHABETICALLY
    ARRANGED
Foster's American Shoe Company
Foster, Lee and Company
Foster's Tailor Shop
Mark L. Foster Corporation
Foster Hardware Store
Foster and Young, Inc.

ALPHABETICALLY
    ARRANGED
Foster Hardware Store
Foster, Lee and Company
Foster, Mark L., Corporation
Foster's American Shoe Company
Foster's Tailor Shop
Foster and Young, Inc.

The numbers in a name should be treated as though they were spelled out:

NOT ALPHABETICALLY
    ARRANGED
4-Deuces Club
2222 Elm Street Building Corp.
18th National Bank

Alphabetically
   Arranged
18th National Bank
4-Deuces Club
2222 Elm Street Building Corp.

When several organizations have the same name, arrange them alphabetically by their locations, considering the town first:

Economy Chevrolet Company,
   Fostoria, Ohio
Economy Chevrolet Company,
   Newmarket, Indiana
Economy Chevrolet Company,
   Newmarket, Wyoming

Names of Government Agencies

The names of government agencies and subdivisions, and officials thereof, are detailed in descending order:

The *Chief of the Bureau of Public Roads of the U.S. Department of Agriculture* should be filed as:

United States Government
Agriculture, Department of,
Public Roads, Bureau of,
. . . ., Chief.

United States Government is the customary heading for agencies of the U.S. Government. Other examples:

U.S. Agricultural Marketing Service should be filed as:

> United States Government
>
> Agriculture, Department of,
>
> Agricultural Marketing Service.

U.S. Employment Service should be filed as:

> United States Government
>
> Commerce, Department of,
>
> Employment Service.

The *Canadian Bureau of Parks and Forests* should be filed as:

> Dominion of Canada
>
> Mines and Resources, Department of,
>
> Parks and Forests, Bureau of.

The *Bureau of Air Pollution Control of the State of Illinois* should be filed as:

> Illinois, State of,
>
> Public Health, Department of,
>
> Air Pollution Control, Bureau of.

The *Bureau of Forestry and Parkways of the City of Chicago* should be filed as:

> Chicago, City of,
>
> Public Works, Department of,
>
> Forestry and Parkways, Bureau of.

Chapter 7

TIME CHANGE

A secretary must often know what time it is in distant cities (for placing telephone calls or making up itineraries, for example). The following list will quickly give you the time in any part of the world.

When all parts of a country are in the same time zone, only the name of the country is given in the list. When there is more than one time zone in a country, the principal cities of that country are listed.

The list is based on the actual time in the Eastern Standard Time zone. If you are in that time zone, you simply add or subtract the number of hours indicated after the name of the country whose time you are seeking. For example, if you are in New York and wish to know what time it is in Denmark, simply look up Denmark in the list and add 6 hours ad indicated.

If you are not in the Eastern Standard Time zone, follow these steps:

a) locate in the list the name of the country or city *where you are;*

b) reverse the sign given (e.g. change "+2" to "−2") and then either add or subtract that number from your actual time;

c) locate the name of the country you are interested in and add or subtract (as indicated) the number from the result of "b."

For example, if you are in Denver and it is 5 PM and you wish to know what time it is in Belgium:

a) locate *Denver* in the list;

b) change "−2" to "+2" and add those 2 hours to your actual time (Denver time is 5 PM + 2 hours = 7 PM);

c) locate Belgium and add, as indicated, 6 hours to the result of "b" (7 PM). The result shows that it is 1 AM in Belgium when it is 5 PM in Denver.

NOTE: Always subtract one hour from the final result when Daylight Saving Time is in effect in your area.

Afghanistan $+9\frac{1}{2}$	Bangladesh $+11$
Algeria $+6$	Barbados $+1$
Argentina $+1$	Belgium $+6$
Australia	Bolivia $+1$
Adelaide $+14\frac{1}{2}$	Botswana $+7$
Brisbane $+15$	Brazil
Canberra $+15$	Belo Horizonte $+2$
Melbourne $+15$	Brasilia $+2$
Perth $+13$	Campo Grande $+1$
Sydney $+15$	Recife $+2$
Austria $+6$	Pôrto Velho $+1$

Rio de Janeiro +2
São Paulo +2
Bulgaria +7
Burma +11½
Burundi +7
Cambodia +12
Cameroon +6
Canada
  Montreal 0
  Ottawa 0
  Toronto 0
  Vancouver −3
  Winnipeg −1
Central Africa
  Republic +6
Chad +6
Chile +1
China +13
Colombia 0
Congo, Rep. of +6
Costa Rica −1
Cuba 0
Cyprus +6
Czechoslovakia +6
Dahomey +6
Denmark +6
Dominican Rep. 0
Ecuador 0
Egypt +7
El Salvador −1
Equatorial
  Guinea +6
Ethiopia +8
Finland +7

France +6
Gabon +6
Gambia +5
Germany, East +6
Germany, West +6
Ghana +5
Greece +7
Guatemala −1
Guinea +5
Guyana +2
Haiti 0
Honduras −1
Hong Kong +13
Hungary +6
Iceland +4
India +10½
Indonesia
  Bandung +12
  Djakarta +12
  Irian Jaya +14
  Semarang +13
  Surabaya +12
Iran +8½
Iraq +8
Ireland +6
Italy +6
Ivory Coast +5
Jamaica 0
Japan +14
Jordan +7
Kenya +8
Korea, North +14
Korea, South +14
Kuwait +8

Laos +12

Lebanon +7

Lesotho +7

Liberia +5¾

Libya +7

Luxembourg +6

Malagasy Rep. +8

Malawi +7

Malasia +12½

Maldive Is. +10

Mali +5

Malta +6

Mauretania +5

Mauritius +9

Mexico

  Guadalajara −1

  Mexico City −1

  Monterey −1

  Mazatlán −2

Mongolian Rep. +13

Morocco +5

Nepal +10½

Netherlands +6

New Zealand +17

Nicaragua −1

Niger +6

Nigeria +6

Pakistan +10

Panama 0

Paraguay +1

Peru 0

Philippines +13

Poland +6

Portugal +6

Rhodesia +7

Rumania +7

Samoa, W. −6

Saudi Arabia +9

Senegal +5

Singapore +12½

Somalia +8

South Africa +7

Spain +6

Sri Lanka +10½

Sudan +7

Sweden +6

Switzerland +6

Syria +7

Taiwan +13

Tanzania +8

Thailand +12

Togo Rep. +5

Trinidad and

  Tobago +1

Tunisia +6

Turkey +7

Uganda +8

USSR

  Alma-Ata +11

  Baku +9

  Gorky +9

  Kharkov +8

  Kiev +8

  Kuibyshev +9

  Leningrad +8

  Minsk +8

  Moscow +8

  Novosibirsk +12

Odessa +8
Omsk +12
Perm +12
Rostov +9
Tashkent +11
Vladivostok +15
Volgograd +9
United Kingdom +6
United States
  Anchorage −5
  Atlanta 0
  Baltimore 0
  Boston 0
  Buffalo 0
  Chicago −1
  Cincinnati 0
  Cleveland 0
  Columbus 0
  Denver −2
  Detroit 0
  Honolulu −5
  Houston −1
  Indianapolis −1
  Kansas City −1

Memphis −1
Minneapolis −1
New York 0
Los Angeles −3
Milwaukee −1
New Orleans −1
Phoenix −2
Pittsburgh 0
Philadelphia 0
St. Louis −1
San Antonio −1
San Francisco −3
Seattle −3
Washington 0
Upper Volta +5
Uruguay +2
Venezuela +1
Vietnam, North +13
Vietnam, South +13
Yemen +8
Yugoslavia +6
Zaire
  Kinshasa +6
  Lumbumbashi +7
Zambia +7

Chapter 8

ROMAN NUMERALS

The following principles and table illustrate the formation of roman numerals:

1. A letter immediately preceding a letter of equal or lesser value adds to it:

    VI = 6; XX = 20; CX = 110

2. A letter immediately preceding a letter of greater value subtracts from it:

    IV = 4; XC = 90; CD = 400

3. A letter occurring between two letters, each of greater value, subtracts from the letter following, the difference then being added to the first letter:

$$
\begin{array}{rl}
XIV &= 14 \\
V &= 5 \\
-I &= -1 \\
+X &= 10 \\
\hline
XIV &= 14 \text{ (since } I \text{ occurs be-} \\
& \quad \text{tween } X \text{ and } V)
\end{array}
$$

$$XLIV = 44$$
$$V = 5$$
$$-I = -1$$
$$\underline{+L = 50}$$

LIV = 54 (since I occurs between L and V)

$$\underline{-X = -10}$$

XLIV = 44 (by rule 2)

$$CDXCIX = 499$$
$$X = 10$$
$$-I = -1$$
$$\underline{+C = 100}$$

CIX = 109 (since I occurs between C and X)

$$-X = -10$$
$$\underline{+D = 500}$$

DXCIX = 599 (since X occurs between D and C)

$$\underline{-C = -100}$$

CDXCIX = 499 (by rule 2)

$$MCM = 1,900$$
$$M = 1,000$$
$$-C = -100$$
$$\underline{+M = 1,000}$$

MCM = 1,900 (since C occurs between M and M)

4. A bar over a letter multiplies it by 1,000:

$$\overline{V} = 5{,}000; \quad \overline{L} = 50{,}000$$

Table of Roman Numerals

Arabic Numeral	Roman Numeral	Arabic Numeral	Roman Numeral
1	I	50	L
2	II	60	LX
3	III	70	LXX
4	IV	80	LXXX
5	V	90	XC
6	VI	100	C
7	VII	200	CC
8	VIII	300	CCC
9	IX	400	CD
10	X	500	D
11	XI	600	DC
12	XII	700	DCC
13	XIII	800	DCCC
14	XIV	900	CM
15	XV	1,000	M
16	XVI	4,000	$M\overline{V}$
17	XVII	5,000	$\overline{V}$
18	XVIII	10,000	$\overline{X}$
19	XIX	15,000	$\overline{XV}$
20	XX	20,000	$\overline{XX}$
30	XXX	100,000	$\overline{C}$
40	XL	1,000,000	$\overline{M}$

Chapter 9

PERPETUAL CALENDAR

This calendar will give you the day of the week on which a date falls during the two centuries from 1901 to the year 2100. To locate the day, first look at the proper year in the list below. A letter follows this year which indicates the calendar in use during that year.

1901	C	1923	B	1945	B	1967	A	1989	A
1902	D	1924	J	1946	C	1968	I	1990	B
1903	E	1925	E	1947	D	1969	D	1991	C
1904	M	1926	F	1948	L	1970	E	1992	K
1905	A	1927	G	1949	G	1971	F	1993	F
1906	B	1928	H	1950	A	1972	N	1994	G
1907	C	1929	C	1951	B	1973	B	1995	A
1908	K	1930	D	1952	J	1974	C	1996	I
1909	F	1931	E	1953	E	1975	D	1997	D
1910	G	1932	M	1954	F	1976	L	1998	E
1911	A	1933	A	1955	G	1977	G	1999	F
1912	I	1934	B	1956	H	1978	A	2000	N
1913	D	1935	C	1957	C	1979	B	2001	B
1914	E	1936	K	1958	D	1980	J	2002	C
1915	F	1937	F	1959	E	1981	E	2003	D
1916	N	1938	G	1960	M	1982	F	2004	L
1917	B	1939	A	1961	A	1983	G	2005	G
1918	C	1940	I	1962	B	1984	H	2006	A
1919	D	1941	D	1963	C	1985	C	2007	B
1920	L	1942	E	1964	K	1986	D	2008	J
1921	G	1943	F	1965	F	1987	E	2009	E
1922	A	1944	N	1966	G	1988	M	2010	F

2011	G	2041	C	2071	E
2012	H	2042	D	2072	M
2013	C	2043	E	2073	A
2014	D	2044	M	2074	B
2015	E	2045	A	2075	C
2016	M	2046	B	2076	K
2017	A	2047	C	2077	F
2018	B	2048	K	2078	G
2019	C	2049	F	2079	A
2020	K	2050	G	2080	I
2021	F	2051	A	2081	D
2022	G	2052	I	2082	E
2023	A	2053	D	2083	F
2024	I	2054	E	2084	N
2025	D	2055	F	2085	B
2026	E	2056	N	2086	C
2027	F	2057	B	2087	D
2028	N	2058	C	2088	L
2029	B	2059	D	2089	G
2030	C	2060	L	2090	A
2031	D	2061	G	2091	B
2032	L	2062	A	2092	J
2033	G	2063	B	2093	E
2034	A	2064	J	2094	F
2035	B	2065	E	2095	G
2036	J	2066	F	2096	H
2037	E	2067	G	2097	C
2038	F	2068	H	2098	D
2039	G	2069	C	2099	E
2040	H	2070	D	2100	F

A

JANUARY	MAY	SEPTEMBER
S M T W T F S	S M T W T F S	S M T W T F S
1 2 3 4 5 6 7	1 2 3 4 5 6	1 2
8 9 10 11 12 13 14	7 8 9 10 11 12 13	3 4 5 6 7 8 9
15 16 17 18 19 20 21	14 15 16 17 18 19 20	10 11 12 13 14 15 16
22 23 24 25 26 27 28	21 22 23 24 25 26 27	17 18 19 20 21 22 23
29 30 31	28 29 30 31	24 25 26 27 28 29 30

FEBRUARY	JUNE	OCTOBER
S M T W T F S	S M T W T F S	S M T W T F S
1 2 3 4	1 2 3	1 2 3 4 5 6 7
5 6 7 8 9 10 11	4 5 6 7 8 9 10	8 9 10 11 12 13 14
12 13 14 15 16 17 18	11 12 13 14 15 16 17	15 16 17 18 19 20 21
19 20 21 22 23 24 25	18 19 20 21 22 23 24	22 23 24 25 26 27 28
26 27 28	25 26 27 28 29 30	29 30 31

MARCH	JULY	NOVEMBER
S M T W T F S	S M T W T F S	S M T W T F S
1 2 3 4	1	1 2 3 4
5 6 7 8 9 10 11	2 3 4 5 6 7 8	5 6 7 8 9 10 11
12 13 14 15 16 17 18	9 10 11 12 13 14 15	12 13 14 15 16 17 18
19 20 21 22 23 24 25	16 17 18 19 20 21 22	19 20 21 22 23 24 25
26 27 28 29 30 31	23 24 25 26 27 28 29	26 27 28 29 30
	30 31	

APRIL	AUGUST	DECEMBER
S M T W T F S	S M T W T F S	S M T W T F S
1	1 2 3 4 5	1 2
2 3 4 5 6 7 8	6 7 8 9 10 11 12	3 4 5 6 7 8 9
9 10 11 12 13 14 15	13 14 15 16 17 18 19	10 11 12 13 14 15 16
16 17 18 19 20 21 22	20 21 22 23 24 25 26	17 18 19 20 21 22 23
23 24 25 26 27 28 29	27 28 29 30 31	24 25 26 27 28 29 30
30		31

B

JANUARY	MAY	SEPTEMBER
S M T W T F S	S M T W T F S	S M T W T F S
1 2 3 4 5 6	1 2 3 4 5	1
7 8 9 10 11 12 13	6 7 8 9 10 11 12	2 3 4 5 6 7 8
14 15 16 17 18 19 20	13 14 15 16 17 18 19	9 10 11 12 13 14 15
21 22 23 24 25 26 27	20 21 22 23 24 25 26	16 17 18 19 20 21 22
28 29 30 31	27 28 29 30 31	23 24 25 26 27 28 29
		30

FEBRUARY	JUNE	OCTOBER
S M T W T F S	S M T W T F S	S M T W T F S
1 2 3	1 2	1 2 3 4 5 6
4 5 6 7 8 9 10	3 4 5 6 7 8 9	7 8 9 10 11 12 13
11 12 13 14 15 16 17	10 11 12 13 14 15 16	14 15 16 17 18 19 20
18 19 20 21 22 23 24	17 18 19 20 21 22 23	21 22 23 24 25 26 27
25 26 27 28	24 25 26 27 28 29 30	28 29 30 31

MARCH	JULY	NOVEMBER
S M T W T F S	S M T W T F S	S M T W T F S
1 2 3	1 2 3 4 5 6 7	1 2 3
4 5 6 7 8 9 10	8 9 10 11 12 13 14	4 5 6 7 8 9 10
11 12 13 14 15 16 17	15 16 17 18 19 20 21	11 12 13 14 15 16 17
18 19 20 21 22 23 24	22 23 24 25 26 27 28	18 19 20 21 22 23 24
25 26 27 28 29 30 31	29 30 31	25 26 27 28 29 30

APRIL	AUGUST	DECEMBER
S M T W T F S	S M T W T F S	S M T W T F S
1 2 3 4 5 6 7	1 2 3 4	1
8 9 10 11 12 13 14	5 6 7 8 9 10 11	2 3 4 5 6 7 8
15 16 17 18 19 20 21	12 13 14 15 16 17 18	9 10 11 12 13 14 15
22 23 24 25 26 27 28	19 20 21 22 23 24 25	16 17 18 19 20 21 22
29 30	26 27 28 29 30 31	23 24 25 26 27 28 29
		30 31

C

JANUARY						
S	M	T	W	T	F	S
		1	2	3	4	5
6	7	8	9	10	11	12
13	14	15	16	17	18	19
20	21	22	23	24	25	26
27	28	29	30	31		

MAY						
S	M	T	W	T	F	S
			1	2	3	4
5	6	7	8	9	10	11
12	13	14	15	16	17	18
19	20	21	22	23	24	25
26	27	28	29	30	31	

SEPTEMBER						
S	M	T	W	T	F	S
1	2	3	4	5	6	7
8	9	10	11	12	13	14
15	16	17	18	19	20	21
22	23	24	25	26	27	28
29	30					

FEBRUARY						
S	M	T	W	T	F	S
					1	2
3	4	5	6	7	8	9
10	11	12	13	14	15	16
17	18	19	20	21	22	23
24	25	26	27	28		

JUNE						
S	M	T	W	T	F	S
						1
2	3	4	5	6	7	8
9	10	11	12	13	14	15
16	17	18	19	20	21	22
23	24	25	26	27	28	29
30						

OCTOBER						
S	M	T	W	T	F	S
		1	2	3	4	5
6	7	8	9	10	11	12
13	14	15	16	17	18	19
20	21	22	23	24	25	26
27	28	29	30	31		

MARCH						
S	M	T	W	T	F	S
					1	2
3	4	5	6	7	8	9
10	11	12	13	14	15	16
17	18	19	20	21	22	23
24	25	26	27	28	29	30
31						

JULY						
S	M	T	W	T	F	S
	1	2	3	4	5	6
7	8	9	10	11	12	13
14	15	16	17	18	19	20
21	22	23	24	25	26	27
28	29	30	31			

NOVEMBER						
S	M	T	W	T	F	S
					1	2
3	4	5	6	7	8	9
10	11	12	13	14	15	16
17	18	19	20	21	22	23
24	25	26	27	28	29	30

APRIL						
S	M	T	W	T	F	S
	1	2	3	4	5	6
7	8	9	10	11	12	13
14	15	16	17	18	19	20
21	22	23	24	25	26	27
28	29	30				

AUGUST						
S	M	T	W	T	F	S
				1	2	3
4	5	6	7	8	9	10
11	12	13	14	15	16	17
18	19	20	21	22	23	24
25	26	27	28	29	30	31

DECEMBER						
S	M	T	W	T	F	S
1	2	3	4	5	6	7
8	9	10	11	12	13	14
15	16	17	18	19	20	21
22	23	24	25	26	27	28
29	30	31				

D

JANUARY						
S	M	T	W	T	F	S
		1	2	3	4	
5	6	7	8	9	10	11
12	13	14	15	16	17	18
19	20	21	22	23	24	25
26	27	28	29	30	31	

MAY						
S	M	T	W	T	F	S
				1	2	3
4	5	6	7	8	9	10
11	12	13	14	15	16	17
18	19	20	21	22	23	24
25	26	27	28	29	30	31

SEPTEMBER						
S	M	T	W	T	F	S
	1	2	3	4	5	6
7	8	9	10	11	12	13
14	15	16	17	18	19	20
21	22	23	24	25	26	27
28	29	30				

FEBRUARY						
S	M	T	W	T	F	S
						1
2	3	4	5	6	7	8
9	10	11	12	13	14	15
16	17	18	19	20	21	22
23	24	25	26	27	28	

JUNE						
S	M	T	W	T	F	S
1	2	3	4	5	6	7
8	9	10	11	12	13	14
15	16	17	18	19	20	21
22	23	24	25	26	27	28
29	30					

OCTOBER						
S	M	T	W	T	F	S
			1	2	3	4
5	6	7	8	9	10	11
12	13	14	15	16	17	18
19	20	21	22	23	24	25
26	27	28	29	30	31	

MARCH						
S	M	T	W	T	F	S
						1
2	3	4	5	6	7	8
9	10	11	12	13	14	15
16	17	18	19	20	21	22
23	24	25	26	27	28	29
30	31					

JULY						
S	M	T	W	T	F	S
		1	2	3	4	5
6	7	8	9	10	11	12
13	14	15	16	17	18	19
20	21	22	23	24	25	26
27	28	29	30	31		

NOVEMBER						
S	M	T	W	T	F	S
						1
2	3	4	5	6	7	8
9	10	11	12	13	14	15
16	17	18	19	20	21	22
23	24	25	26	27	28	29
30						

APRIL						
S	M	T	W	T	F	S
		1	2	3	4	5
6	7	8	9	10	11	12
13	14	15	16	17	18	19
20	21	22	23	24	25	26
27	28	29	30			

AUGUST						
S	M	T	W	T	F	S
					1	2
3	4	5	6	7	8	9
10	11	12	13	14	15	16
17	18	19	20	21	22	23
24	25	26	27	28	29	30
31						

DECEMBER						
S	M	T	W	T	F	S
	1	2	3	4	5	6
7	8	9	10	11	12	13
14	15	16	17	18	19	20
21	22	23	24	25	26	27
28	29	30	31			

PERPETUAL CALENDAR

E

JANUARY
S	M	T	W	T	F	S
				1	2	3
4	5	6	7	8	9	10
11	12	13	14	15	16	17
18	19	20	21	22	23	24
25	26	27	28	29	30	31

MAY
S	M	T	W	T	F	S
					1	2
3	4	5	6	7	8	9
10	11	12	13	14	15	16
17	18	19	20	21	22	23
24	25	26	27	28	29	30
31						

SEPTEMBER
S	M	T	W	T	F	S
		1	2	3	4	5
6	7	8	9	10	11	12
13	14	15	16	17	18	19
20	21	22	23	24	25	26
27	28	29	30			

FEBRUARY
S	M	T	W	T	F	S
1	2	3	4	5	6	7
8	9	10	11	12	13	14
15	16	17	18	19	20	21
22	23	24	25	26	27	28

JUNE
S	M	T	W	T	F	S
	1	2	3	4	5	6
7	8	9	10	11	12	13
14	15	16	17	18	19	20
21	22	23	24	25	26	27
28	29	30				

OCTOBER
S	M	T	W	T	F	S
				1	2	3
4	5	6	7	8	9	10
11	12	13	14	15	16	17
18	19	20	21	22	23	24
25	26	27	28	29	30	31

MARCH
S	M	T	W	T	F	S
1	2	3	4	5	6	7
8	9	10	11	12	13	14
15	16	17	18	19	20	21
22	23	24	25	26	27	28
29	30	31				

JULY
S	M	T	W	T	F	S
			1	2	3	4
5	6	7	8	9	10	11
12	13	14	15	16	17	18
19	20	21	22	23	24	25
26	27	28	29	30	31	

NOVEMBER
S	M	T	W	T	F	S
1	2	3	4	5	6	7
8	9	10	11	12	13	14
15	16	17	18	19	20	21
22	23	24	25	26	27	28
29	30					

APRIL
S	M	T	W	T	F	S
			1	2	3	4
5	6	7	8	9	10	11
12	13	14	15	16	17	18
19	20	21	22	23	24	25
26	27	28	29	30		

AUGUST
S	M	T	W	T	F	S
						1
2	3	4	5	6	7	8
9	10	11	12	13	14	15
16	17	18	19	20	21	22
23	24	25	26	27	28	29
30	31					

DECEMBER
S	M	T	W	T	F	S
		1	2	3	4	5
6	7	8	9	10	11	12
13	14	15	16	17	18	19
20	21	22	23	24	25	26
27	28	29	30	31		

F

JANUARY
S	M	T	W	T	F	S
					1	2
3	4	5	6	7	8	9
10	11	12	13	14	15	16
17	18	19	20	21	22	23
24	25	26	27	28	29	30
31						

MAY
S	M	T	W	T	F	S
						1
2	3	4	5	6	7	8
9	10	11	12	13	14	15
16	17	18	19	20	21	22
23	24	25	26	27	28	29
30	31					

SEPTEMBER
S	M	T	W	T	F	S
			1	2	3	4
5	6	7	8	9	10	11
12	13	14	15	16	17	18
19	20	21	22	23	24	25
26	27	28	29	30		

FEBRUARY
S	M	T	W	T	F	S
	1	2	3	4	5	6
7	8	9	10	11	12	13
14	15	16	17	18	19	20
21	22	23	24	25	26	27
28						

JUNE
S	M	T	W	T	F	S
		1	2	3	4	5
6	7	8	9	10	11	12
13	14	15	16	17	18	19
20	21	22	23	24	25	26
27	28	29	30			

OCTOBER
S	M	T	W	T	F	S
					1	2
3	4	5	6	7	8	9
10	11	12	13	14	15	16
17	18	19	20	21	22	23
24	25	26	27	28	29	30
31						

MARCH
S	M	T	W	T	F	S
	1	2	3	4	5	6
7	8	9	10	11	12	13
14	15	16	17	18	19	20
21	22	23	24	25	26	27
28	29	30	31			

JULY
S	M	T	W	T	F	S
				1	2	3
4	5	6	7	8	9	10
11	12	13	14	15	16	17
18	19	20	21	22	23	24
25	26	27	28	29	30	31

NOVEMBER
S	M	T	W	T	F	S
	1	2	3	4	5	6
7	8	9	10	11	12	13
14	15	16	17	18	19	20
21	22	23	24	25	26	27
28	29	30				

APRIL
S	M	T	W	T	F	S
				1	2	3
4	5	6	7	8	9	10
11	12	13	14	15	16	17
18	19	20	21	22	23	24
25	26	27	28	29	30	

AUGUST
S	M	T	W	T	F	S
1	2	3	4	5	6	7
8	9	10	11	12	13	14
15	16	17	18	19	20	21
22	23	24	25	26	27	28
29	30	31				

DECEMBER
S	M	T	W	T	F	S
			1	2	3	4
5	6	7	8	9	10	11
12	13	14	15	16	17	18
19	20	21	22	23	24	25
26	27	28	29	30	31	

G

JANUARY
S	M	T	W	T	F	S
						1
2	3	4	5	6	7	8
9	10	11	12	13	14	15
16	17	18	19	20	21	22
23	24	25	26	27	28	29
30	31					

MAY
S	M	T	W	T	F	S
1	2	3	4	5	6	7
8	9	10	11	12	13	14
15	16	17	18	19	20	21
22	23	24	25	26	27	28
29	30	31				

SEPTEMBER
S	M	T	W	T	F	S
					1	2	3
4	5	6	7	8	9	10
11	12	13	14	15	16	17
18	19	20	21	22	23	24
25	26	27	28	29	30	

FEBRUARY
S	M	T	W	T	F	S
		1	2	3	4	5
6	7	8	9	10	11	12
13	14	15	16	17	18	19
20	21	22	23	24	25	26
27	28					

JUNE
S	M	T	W	T	F	S
			1	2	3	4
5	6	7	8	9	10	11
12	13	14	15	16	17	18
19	20	21	22	23	24	25
26	27	28	29	30		

OCTOBER
S	M	T	W	T	F	S
						1
2	3	4	5	6	7	8
9	10	11	12	13	14	15
16	17	18	19	20	21	22
23	24	25	26	27	28	29
30	31					

MARCH
S	M	T	W	T	F	S
		1	2	3	4	5
6	7	8	9	10	11	12
13	14	15	16	17	18	19
20	21	22	23	24	25	26
27	28	29	30	31		

JULY
S	M	T	W	T	F	S
					1	2
3	4	5	6	7	8	9
10	11	12	13	14	15	16
17	18	19	20	21	22	23
24	25	26	27	28	29	30
31						

NOVEMBER
S	M	T	W	T	F	S
		1	2	3	4	5
6	7	8	9	10	11	12
13	14	15	16	17	18	19
20	21	22	23	24	25	26
27	28	29	30			

APRIL
S	M	T	W	T	F	S
					1	2
3	4	5	6	7	8	9
10	11	12	13	14	15	16
17	18	19	20	21	22	23
24	25	26	27	28	29	30

AUGUST
S	M	T	W	T	F	S
	1	2	3	4	5	6
7	8	9	10	11	12	13
14	15	16	17	18	19	20
21	22	23	24	25	26	27
28	29	30	31			

DECEMBER
S	M	T	W	T	F	S
				1	2	3
4	5	6	7	8	9	10
11	12	13	14	15	16	17
18	19	20	21	22	23	24
25	26	27	28	29	30	31

H

JANUARY
S	M	T	W	T	F	S
1	2	3	4	5	6	7
8	9	10	11	12	13	14
15	16	17	18	19	20	21
22	23	24	25	26	27	28
29	30	31				

MAY
S	M	T	W	T	F	S
	1	2	3	4	5	
6	7	8	9	10	11	12
13	14	15	16	17	18	19
20	21	22	23	24	25	26
27	28	29	30	31		

SEPTEMBER
S	M	T	W	T	F	S
						1
2	3	4	5	6	7	8
9	10	11	12	13	14	15
16	17	18	19	20	21	22
23	24	25	26	27	28	29
30						

FEBRUARY
S	M	T	W	T	F	S
			1	2	3	4
5	6	7	8	9	10	11
12	13	14	15	16	17	18
19	20	21	22	23	24	25
26	27	28	29			

JUNE
S	M	T	W	T	F	S
					1	2
3	4	5	6	7	8	9
10	11	12	13	14	15	16
17	18	19	20	21	22	23
24	25	26	27	28	29	30

OCTOBER
S	M	T	W	T	F	S
1	2	3	4	5	6	
7	8	9	10	11	12	13
14	15	16	17	18	19	20
21	22	23	24	25	26	27
28	29	30	31			

MARCH
S	M	T	W	T	F	S
				1	2	3
4	5	6	7	8	9	10
11	12	13	14	15	16	17
18	19	20	21	22	23	24
25	26	27	28	29	30	31

JULY
S	M	T	W	T	F	S
1	2	3	4	5	6	7
8	9	10	11	12	13	14
15	16	17	18	19	20	21
22	23	24	25	26	27	28
29	30	31				

NOVEMBER
S	M	T	W	T	F	S
				1	2	3
4	5	6	7	8	9	10
11	12	13	14	15	16	17
18	19	20	21	22	23	24
25	26	27	28	29	30	

APRIL
S	M	T	W	T	F	S
1	2	3	4	5	6	7
8	9	10	11	12	13	14
15	16	17	18	19	20	21
22	23	24	25	26	27	28
29	30					

AUGUST
S	M	T	W	T	F	S
		1	2	3	4	
5	6	7	8	9	10	11
12	13	14	15	16	17	18
19	20	21	22	23	24	25
26	27	28	29	30	31	

DECEMBER
S	M	T	W	T	F	S
						1
2	3	4	5	6	7	8
9	10	11	12	13	14	15
16	17	18	19	20	21	22
23	24	25	26	27	28	29
30	31					

I

JANUARY

S	M	T	W	T	F	S
	1	2	3	4	5	6
7	8	9	10	11	12	13
14	15	16	17	18	19	20
21	22	23	24	25	26	27
28	29	30	31			

FEBRUARY

S	M	T	W	T	F	S
				1	2	3
4	5	6	7	8	9	10
11	12	13	14	15	16	17
18	19	20	21	22	23	24
25	26	27	28	29		

MARCH

S	M	T	W	T	F	S
					1	2
3	4	5	6	7	8	9
10	11	12	13	14	15	16
17	18	19	20	21	22	23
24	25	26	27	28	29	30
31						

APRIL

S	M	T	W	T	F	S
	1	2	3	4	5	6
7	8	9	10	11	12	13
14	15	16	17	18	19	20
21	22	23	24	25	26	27
28	29	30				

MAY

S	M	T	W	T	F	S
			1	2	3	4
5	6	7	8	9	10	11
12	13	14	15	16	17	18
19	20	21	22	23	24	25
26	27	28	29	30	31	

JUNE

S	M	T	W	T	F	S
						1
2	3	4	5	6	7	8
9	10	11	12	13	14	15
16	17	18	19	20	21	22
23	24	25	26	27	28	29
30						

JULY

S	M	T	W	T	F	S
	1	2	3	4	5	6
7	8	9	10	11	12	13
14	15	16	17	18	19	20
21	22	23	24	25	26	27
28	29	30	31			

AUGUST

S	M	T	W	T	F	S
				1	2	3
4	5	6	7	8	9	10
11	12	13	14	15	16	17
18	19	20	21	22	23	24
25	26	27	28	29	30	31

SEPTEMBER

S	M	T	W	T	F	S
1	2	3	4	5	6	7
8	9	10	11	12	13	14
15	16	17	18	19	20	21
22	23	24	25	26	27	28
29	30					

OCTOBER

S	M	T	W	T	F	S
		1	2	3	4	5
6	7	8	9	10	11	12
13	14	15	16	17	18	19
20	21	22	23	24	25	26
27	28	29	30	31		

NOVEMBER

S	M	T	W	T	F	S
					1	2
3	4	5	6	7	8	9
10	11	12	13	14	15	16
17	18	19	20	21	22	23
24	25	26	27	28	29	30

DECEMBER

S	M	T	W	T	F	S
1	2	3	4	5	6	7
8	9	10	11	12	13	14
15	16	17	18	19	20	21
22	23	24	25	26	27	28
29	30	31				

J

JANUARY

S	M	T	W	T	F	S
		1	2	3	4	5
6	7	8	9	10	11	12
13	14	15	16	17	18	19
20	21	22	23	24	25	26
27	28	29	30	31		

FEBRUARY

S	M	T	W	T	F	S
					1	2
3	4	5	6	7	8	9
10	11	12	13	14	15	16
17	18	19	20	21	22	23
24	25	26	27	28	29	

MARCH

S	M	T	W	T	F	S
						1
2	3	4	5	6	7	8
9	10	11	12	13	14	15
16	17	18	19	20	21	22
23	24	25	26	27	28	29
30	31					

APRIL

S	M	T	W	T	F	S
		1	2	3	4	5
6	7	8	9	10	11	12
13	14	15	16	17	18	19
20	21	22	23	24	25	26
27	28	29	30			

MAY

S	M	T	W	T	F	S
				1	2	3
4	5	6	7	8	9	10
11	12	13	14	15	16	17
18	19	20	21	22	23	24
25	26	27	28	29	30	31

JUNE

S	M	T	W	T	F	S
1	2	3	4	5	6	7
8	9	10	11	12	13	14
15	16	17	18	19	20	21
22	23	24	25	26	27	28
29	30					

JULY

S	M	T	W	T	F	S
		1	2	3	4	5
6	7	8	9	10	11	12
13	14	15	16	17	18	19
20	21	22	23	24	25	26
27	28	29	30	31		

AUGUST

S	M	T	W	T	F	S
					1	2
3	4	5	6	7	8	9
10	11	12	13	14	15	16
17	18	19	20	21	22	23
24	25	26	27	28	29	30
31						

SEPTEMBER

S	M	T	W	T	F	S
	1	2	3	4	5	6
7	8	9	10	11	12	13
14	15	16	17	18	19	20
21	22	23	24	25	26	27
28	29	30				

OCTOBER

S	M	T	W	T	F	S
			1	2	3	4
5	6	7	8	9	10	11
12	13	14	15	16	17	18
19	20	21	22	23	24	25
26	27	28	29	30	31	

NOVEMBER

S	M	T	W	T	F	S
						1
2	3	4	5	6	7	8
9	10	11	12	13	14	15
16	17	18	19	20	21	22
23	24	25	26	27	28	29
30						

DECEMBER

S	M	T	W	T	F	S
	1	2	3	4	5	6
7	8	9	10	11	12	13
14	15	16	17	18	19	20
21	22	23	24	25	26	27
28	29	30	31			

K

JANUARY								MAY								SEPTEMBER						
S	M	T	W	T	F	S		S	M	T	W	T	F	S		S	M	T	W	T	F	S
		1	2	3	4						1	2				1	2	3	4	5		
5	6	7	8	9	10	11		3	4	5	6	7	8	9		6	7	8	9	10	11	12
12	13	14	15	16	17	18		10	11	12	13	14	15	16		13	14	15	16	17	18	19
19	20	21	22	23	24	25		17	18	19	20	21	22	23		20	21	22	23	24	25	26
26	27	28	29	30	31			24	25	26	27	28	29	30		27	28	29	30			
								31														

FEBRUARY								JUNE								OCTOBER						
S	M	T	W	T	F	S		S	M	T	W	T	F	S		S	M	T	W	T	F	S
						1		1	2	3	4	5	6						1	2	3
2	3	4	5	6	7	8		7	8	9	10	11	12	13		4	5	6	7	8	9	10
9	10	11	12	13	14	15		14	15	16	17	18	19	20		11	12	13	14	15	16	17
16	17	18	19	20	21	22		21	22	23	24	25	26	27		18	19	20	21	22	23	24
23	24	25	26	27	28	29		28	29	30						25	26	27	28	29	30	31

MARCH								JULY								NOVEMBER						
S	M	T	W	T	F	S		S	M	T	W	T	F	S		S	M	T	W	T	F	S
1	2	3	4	5	6	7				1	2	3	4			1	2	3	4	5	6	7
8	9	10	11	12	13	14		5	6	7	8	9	10	11		8	9	10	11	12	13	14
15	16	17	18	19	20	21		12	13	14	15	16	17	18		15	16	17	18	19	20	21
22	23	24	25	26	27	28		19	20	21	22	23	24	25		22	23	24	25	26	27	28
29	30	31						26	27	28	29	30	31			29	30					

APRIL								AUGUST								DECEMBER						
S	M	T	W	T	F	S		S	M	T	W	T	F	S		S	M	T	W	T	F	S
		1	2	3	4									1				1	2	3	4	5
5	6	7	8	9	10	11		2	3	4	5	6	7	8		6	7	8	9	10	11	12
12	13	14	15	16	17	18		9	10	11	12	13	14	15		13	14	15	16	17	18	19
19	20	21	22	23	24	25		16	17	18	19	20	21	22		20	21	22	23	24	25	26
26	27	28	29	30				23	24	25	26	27	28	29		27	28	29	30	31		
								30	31													

L

JANUARY								MAY								SEPTEMBER						
S	M	T	W	T	F	S		S	M	T	W	T	F	S		S	M	T	W	T	F	S
				1	2	3								1				1	2	3	4	
4	5	6	7	8	9	10		2	3	4	5	6	7	8		5	6	7	8	9	10	11
11	12	13	14	15	16	17		9	10	11	12	13	14	15		12	13	14	15	16	17	18
18	19	20	21	22	23	24		16	17	18	19	20	21	22		19	20	21	22	23	24	25
25	26	27	28	29	30	31		23	24	25	26	27	28	29		26	27	28	29	30		
								30	31													

FEBRUARY								JUNE								OCTOBER						
S	M	T	W	T	F	S		S	M	T	W	T	F	S		S	M	T	W	T	F	S
1	2	3	4	5	6	7				1	2	3	4	5							1	2
8	9	10	11	12	13	14		6	7	8	9	10	11	12		3	4	5	6	7	8	9
15	16	17	18	19	20	21		13	14	15	16	17	18	19		10	11	12	13	14	15	16
22	23	24	25	26	27	28		20	21	22	23	24	25	26		17	18	19	20	21	22	23
29								27	28	29	30					24	25	26	27	28	29	30
																31						

MARCH								JULY								NOVEMBER						
S	M	T	W	T	F	S		S	M	T	W	T	F	S		S	M	T	W	T	F	S
	1	2	3	4	5	6					1	2	3			1	2	3	4	5	6	
7	8	9	10	11	12	13		4	5	6	7	8	9	10		7	8	9	10	11	12	13
14	15	16	17	18	19	20		11	12	13	14	15	16	17		14	15	16	17	18	19	20
21	22	23	24	25	26	27		18	19	20	21	22	23	24		21	22	23	24	25	26	27
28	29	30	31					25	26	27	28	29	30	31		28	29	30				

APRIL								AUGUST								DECEMBER						
S	M	T	W	T	F	S		S	M	T	W	T	F	S		S	M	T	W	T	F	S
				1	2	3		1	2	3	4	5	6	7				1	2	3	4	
4	5	6	7	8	9	10		8	9	10	11	12	13	14		5	6	7	8	9	10	11
11	12	13	14	15	16	17		15	16	17	18	19	20	21		12	13	14	15	16	17	18
18	19	20	21	22	23	24		22	23	24	25	26	27	28		19	20	21	22	23	24	25
25	26	27	28	29	30			29	30	31						26	27	28	29	30	31	

M

JANUARY
S	M	T	W	T	F	S
					1	2
3	4	5	6	7	8	9
10	11	12	13	14	15	16
17	18	19	20	21	22	23
24	25	26	27	28	29	30
31						

MAY
S	M	T	W	T	F	S
1	2	3	4	5	6	7
8	9	10	11	12	13	14
15	16	17	18	19	20	21
22	23	24	25	26	27	28
29	30	31				

SEPTEMBER
S	M	T	W	T	F	S
				1	2	3
4	5	6	7	8	9	10
11	12	13	14	15	16	17
18	19	20	21	22	23	24
25	26	27	28	29	30	

FEBRUARY
S	M	T	W	T	F	S
	1	2	3	4	5	6
7	8	9	10	11	12	13
14	15	16	17	18	19	20
21	22	23	24	25	26	27
28	29					

JUNE
S	M	T	W	T	F	S
			1	2	3	4
5	6	7	8	9	10	11
12	13	14	15	16	17	18
19	20	21	22	23	24	25
26	27	28	29	30		

OCTOBER
S	M	T	W	T	F	S
						1
2	3	4	5	6	7	8
9	10	11	12	13	14	15
16	17	18	19	20	21	22
23	24	25	26	27	28	29
30	31					

MARCH
S	M	T	W	T	F	S
		1	2	3	4	5
6	7	8	9	10	11	12
13	14	15	16	17	18	19
20	21	22	23	24	25	26
27	28	29	30	31		

JULY
S	M	T	W	T	F	S
					1	2
3	4	5	6	7	8	9
10	11	12	13	14	15	16
17	18	19	20	21	22	23
24	25	26	27	28	29	30
31						

NOVEMBER
S	M	T	W	T	F	S
		1	2	3	4	5
6	7	8	9	10	11	12
13	14	15	16	17	18	19
20	21	22	23	24	25	26
27	28	29	30			

APRIL
S	M	T	W	T	F	S
					1	2
3	4	5	6	7	8	9
10	11	12	13	14	15	16
17	18	19	20	21	22	23
24	25	26	27	28	29	30

AUGUST
S	M	T	W	T	F	S
	1	2	3	4	5	6
7	8	9	10	11	12	13
14	15	16	17	18	19	20
21	22	23	24	25	26	27
28	29	30	31			

DECEMBER
S	M	T	W	T	F	S
				1	2	3
4	5	6	7	8	9	10
11	12	13	14	15	16	17
18	19	20	21	22	23	24
25	26	27	28	29	30	31

N

JANUARY
S	M	T	W	T	F	S
						1
2	3	4	5	6	7	8
9	10	11	12	13	14	15
16	17	18	19	20	21	22
23	24	25	26	27	28	29
30	31					

MAY
S	M	T	W	T	F	S
	1	2	3	4	5	6
7	8	9	10	11	12	13
14	15	16	17	18	19	20
21	22	23	24	25	26	27
28	29	30	31			

SEPTEMBER
S	M	T	W	T	F	S
					1	2
3	4	5	6	7	8	9
10	11	12	13	14	15	16
17	18	19	20	21	22	23
24	25	26	27	28	29	30

FEBRUARY
S	M	T	W	T	F	S
		1	2	3	4	5
6	7	8	9	10	11	12
13	14	15	16	17	18	19
20	21	22	23	24	25	26
27	28	29				

JUNE
S	M	T	W	T	F	S
				1	2	3
4	5	6	7	8	9	10
11	12	13	14	15	16	17
18	19	20	21	22	23	24
25	26	27	28	29	30	

OCTOBER
S	M	T	W	T	F	S
1	2	3	4	5	6	7
8	9	10	11	12	13	14
15	16	17	18	19	20	21
22	23	24	25	26	27	28
29	30	31				

MARCH
S	M	T	W	T	F	S
			1	2	3	4
5	6	7	8	9	10	11
12	13	14	15	16	17	18
19	20	21	22	23	24	25
26	27	28	29	30	31	

JULY
S	M	T	W	T	F	S
						1
2	3	4	5	6	7	8
9	10	11	12	13	14	15
16	17	18	19	20	21	22
23	24	25	26	27	28	29
30	31					

NOVEMBER
S	M	T	W	T	F	S
			1	2	3	4
5	6	7	8	9	10	11
12	13	14	15	16	17	18
19	20	21	22	23	24	25
26	27	28	29	30		

APRIL
S	M	T	W	T	F	S
						1
2	3	4	5	6	7	8
9	10	11	12	13	14	15
16	17	18	19	20	21	22
23	24	25	26	27	28	29
30						

AUGUST
S	M	T	W	T	F	S
		1	2	3	4	5
6	7	8	9	10	11	12
13	14	15	16	17	18	19
20	21	22	23	24	25	26
27	28	29	30	31		

DECEMBER
S	M	T	W	T	F	S
					1	2
3	4	5	6	7	8	9
10	11	12	13	14	15	16
17	18	19	20	21	22	23
24	25	26	27	28	29	30
31						

Chapter 10

PUNCTUATION

Punctuation in written material is often as important as the correct placement of signs and symbols in mathematical calculations. The proper placement of commas, periods, and other punctuation makes the difference between a clear, well-constructed statement and a muddled one. Following are the basic rules for proper punctuation.

Period

1. A period (.) is placed at the end of declarative and imperative sentences and after abbreviations and initials:

Send a letter to Mr. D. M. Green.

Hand me a 1½ in. nail.

2. No period is used at the end of a sentence contained within a longer sentence:

The defendant's reply, "I never saw this man before," surprised everyone.

3. A period is placed after numbers or letters which precede items in a list:

1. the early period before 1800
b. parrots and their allies

Question Mark

4. A question mark (?) is placed after a direct question:

Where will you be this summer?

5. A question mark follows an interrogative sentence even when part of a larger sentence:

How can this be done? I wondered.

6. If intended interrogatively, a declarative or imperative sentence ends with a question mark:

This is what we've been waiting for?

7. A question mark is not used after an indirect question:

He asked how long we'd be staying.

8. A question mark enclosed in parentheses is used to indicate uncertainty:

He said he'll be back on May 5 (?).

Exclamation Point

9. An exclamation point (!) is used after interjections and at the end of a sentence for emphasis or to indicate strong emotion:

Aha! I caught you!
That's incredible!

Apostrophe

10. An apostrophe (') is used in contractions to indicate omitted letters or words, and in dates to indicate omitted numerals.

I've never heard of him.
Come at eight o'clock.
He graduated in '46.

11. An apostrophe with an *s* ('s) is added to form the possessive case of most singular nouns; exceptions are such words as *conscience, righteousness,* etc., and certain ancient or Biblical names, which take an apostrophe without *s.*

man's hat
horse's stable
Marx's theories
Strauss's waltz
appearance' sake
Moses' tablet

12. An apostrophe only is added to form the possessive case of plural nouns ending in *s;* plural nouns not ending in *s* take an apostrophe with *s:*

boys' fathers
men's ties
geese's grain
the Joneses' estates

13. An apostrophe with *s* is added to form the possessive case of indefinite pronouns not ending in *s;* indefinite pronouns ending in *s* take an apostrophe only:

somebody's scarf
others' rights

14. An apostrophe with *s* is used to form the plural of letters, signs, symbols, and numbers; plurals of years, however, are commonly formed with *s* alone:

"Occurred" is spelled with two "r's."

The number is followed by four "8's."

the 1890s (or 1890's)

Quotation Marks

15. Quotation marks (" ") are used to enclose direct quotations, ironic and slang expressions, nicknames, titles of short works, and sections of longer works:

Peter cried, "Let's go!"

"When," the children asked, "are we going to the circus?"

Our "leader," it seems, had vanished.

William H. Bonney was known as "Billy the Kid."

Chapter 2 is titled "Ancient Music."

He sang "The Wanderer," by Schubert.

16. Quotation marks enclose words, phrases, etc., referred to in a sentence:

The words "once upon a time" are used to begin many children's stories.

17. Single quotation marks (' ') enclose quotations within quotations:

"I think," Steve replied, "that George said, 'No, I am not going.'"

"Spell 'leisure,'" he ordered.

18. Single quotation marks are often used to enclose philosophical and theological terms that have a special meaning:

'beatific vision'

Ellipsis Points

19. Ellipsis points(. . . .) are used to indicate material which has been omitted from a quoted passage. Use three dots to indicate an omission within a sentence; punctuation marks may be retained on either side of the ellipsis, but this is optional:

Samuel Johnson said, "Praise . . . owes its value only to its scarcity."

20. Use four dots—a period followed by three dots—if the omitted material is (1) the end of a sentence, (2) the beginning of the next sentence, (3) the whole next sentence, or (4) the next paragraph or more. If the sentence ends with a question mark or exclamation point, use this punctuation followed by three dots. If the beginning of a sentence is omitted, the sentence will usually begin with a lower-case letter:

In *Walden* Thoreau observed: "Public opinion is a weak tyrant. . . . What a man thinks of himself . . . determines his fate."

As Shaw remarked, "Liberty means responsibility. . . . most men dread it."

Comma

21. Use commas (,) to set off a series of three or more items joined by *and, or,* or *nor. Etc.,* when used, should be set off by commas:

> Marcia, Tony, and Judy went downtown.

> Pins, earrings, lockets, etc., are on sale this month.

22. Do not use commas if the items are joined by conjunctions and are relatively simple:

> I don't know whether to divide by 2 or 3 or 6.

23. Use a comma to set off a direct quotation:

> "It's a terrible book," he said.

> John asked, "How much does it cost?"

24. A quotation which is the subject or predicate nominative of a sentence is not set off by a comma:

> "We shall overcome" was his motto.

> His motto was "We shall overcome."

25. Titles following a proper name are set off by commas:

> James Horton, president of Acme Corporation, is on the committee.

26. Appositives are set off by commas:

> The janitor, Mr. Brown, is sick today.

27. Words of direct address and interjections are set off by commas:

> "Charles, go to the back door."

> Well, we must try another method.

28. Two or more adjectives preceding a noun are separated by commas, except when the adjective and noun are a unit:

> We had a short, rainy spring last year.

> All the large electric lights were out.

29. Two or more phrases referring to a single following word are separated by commas:

> These shocking, though not unexpected, events could lead to panic.

30. Use commas before conjunctions joining two independent clauses in compound sentences, except when the clauses are short and closely related:

> That is an interesting city, but it's too crowded to appeal to me.

> Tom walked down the road and his brother followed him.

31. Dependent clauses or participial phrases at the beginning of a sentence are set off by commas, unless a part of the verb:

> Although we advised her not to, she went to California.

> Walking beside the road was an old man.

32. Dependent clauses at the end of a sentence are set off by commas if not essential to the basic meaning of the sentence:

> She went to California, although we advised her not to.

We finally agreed to return if we could meet again next week.

33. Introductory adverbial phrases, unless quite brief, are followed by a comma except when they immediately precede the verb:

While closing the curtains, she noticed a man walking past.

After dinner we went for a walk.

Into the room rushed several dogs.

34. Adverbial clauses or phrases between subject and verb are set off by commas:

Barton, after consulting with several authorities, proposed changes.

35. An adjectival clause or phrase is set off by commas if dropping it would not change the meaning of the noun:

The winning bicycle, which weighed only 12 pounds, was made in France.

36. A parenthetical clause, phrase, or word is set off by commas:

This month there have been, as far as we know, two accidents.

37. Expressions such as "however," "therefore," "after all," etc., are set off by commas if they break the continuity of thought. If they do not break the continuity or require a pause, commas should not be used:

The answer, perhaps, is to send out a questionnaire.

I therefore demand that you remain.

Comma (Special Uses)

38. Inverted names, as in a list, have a comma between the last and first name:

Whitman, Walt

Whittier, John Greenleaf

39. Words which together might be misunderstood or awkward to read are separated by commas:

Where he is, is not known.

To Frank, Jones was most polite.

40. Expressions such as *i.e., namely,* and *that is* are set off by commas; sometimes a semicolon or other punctuation precedes:

The discussion centered on the ancient Greek tragic playwrights, i.e., Aeschylus, Sophocles, and Euripides.

The ruling applies only to part-time employees; that is, employees working less than thirty hours weekly.

41. Interrelated contrasting clauses should be separated by a comma:

The bigger they are, the harder they fall.

42. Words which are omitted but understood in context are indicated by the use of a comma:

He had a thousand friends when he was rich; when poor, none.

43. A comma is used to separate an

interrogative clause from a declarative clause that it follows:

> You'll be here tomorrow night, won't you?

44. The parts of addresses are separated by commas:

> He lives at 1414 Whitehall Drive, Brighton, Maryland.

45. Commas are used in dates as follows:

> On September 12, 1959, the . . .
> Thursday, April 25, is . . .
> June 1947 (*no comma*)
> 12 September 1959 (*no comma*)

46. In numbers of four or more digits, use commas to separate thousands, millions, etc. Commas are not used in ZIP codes, phone numbers, page or serial numbers.

> 3,421 miles
> a population of 20,590,120
> page 2189
> Chicago, Ill. 60602

47. A comma is used to separate two sets of figures:

> In 1940, 159 people died of that disease.

Colon

48. A colon (:) is used to introduce series or lists:

> Questionnaires were mailed to three states: Maine, Iowa, and Florida.

The steps are as follows:
1. Construct a triangle. . . .
2. Connect points. . . .

49. A complete sentence, question, or long quotation is introduced by a colon:

One rule is paramount: Do not fire until the order is given.

I quote from his recent speech: "In times such as ours . . . caution is our best policy. . . ."

50. A colon is used to introduce speech in a dialog, and following the introductory address of a speaker:

Father: Has he asked you to marry him?

Julie: Oh no, he . . .

Ladies and Gentlemen:

51. Colons are used to punctuate time indications, Bible references, volume and page references, and ratios as follows (many Catholic Bibles, however, now have a comma in place of a colon):

at exactly 3:48 in the afternoon
I Kings 1:20 (or I Kings 1,20)
American Psychologist 10:17-25
in the ratio of 7:5

Semicolon

52. Items in a series are separated by a semicolon (;) when the items contain a comma or other internal punctuation:

The number of games played this

season is: team A, 3; team B, 5; team C, 2.

53. Two independent clauses which are not joined by a conjunction are separated by a semicolon:

The old buildings I liked; the new ones were atrocious.

54. If the clauses of a compound sentence are long or internally punctuated, a semicolon is used between them, before the conjunction:

The girls, who had been waiting hours for a chance to see their idol, pressed eagerly forward when he appeared; but their disappointment was great when he swiftly darted into the nearest cab without even acknowledging their presence.

55. A semicolon is used between the independent parts of a sentence that contain commas indicating omitted words:

In Illinois we have thirteen delegates; in Indiana, nine; in Iowa, eight.

Dash

56. A dash (—) is used to indicate a sudden break in thought:

He said—to everyone's amazement— that the Chinese were crossing the border.

57. Dashes may be used to set off a

phrase or word repeated for emphasis:

> That is the price for one volume—one volume only—not for the set.

58. An unfinished word or sentence is indicated by the use of a dash:

> "I'm going to snee—," she cried.

59. A phrase which introduces a series and is understood to be repeated before each item is followed by a dash:

> The committee decided—
>   1. to change the date of meeting;
>   2. to increase the dues;
>   3. to hold new elections.

60. Dashes may be used in place of commas to clarify the meaning of a sentence:

> The basic ingredients of a cake—flour, sugar, milk, and eggs—were ready.

61. A final clause summarizing a series of ideas in a sentence, or which is an expansion of something in the main clause, is set off by a dash:

> I always use the dictionary, the thesaurus, and a grammar—three indispensable aids when writing.
>
> After lunch we toured the caves—the same caves where three men had died.

62. A short dash(-) is used to indicate inclusive or continuing numbers, dates, etc. Do not use with such words as *from* and *between*:

> the period 1952–59

11:A.M.–9:00 P.M.
pp. 197–210
Sept. 25, 1962–June 6, 1963
from 1952 to 1959 (*not* from 1952–59)

Parentheses

63. An independent part of a sentence
or paragraph not directly related to the
main statement is enclosed in parentheses [( )]:

> Three people (all in the last row) were
> snoring loudly.

> The pool will be open until Labor
> Day. (Last year it closed August 20.)

64. Parentheses are used to enclose letters or numbers enumerating items in a
series, or with numerals or other symbols used appositively:

> He traced the development of the
> symphony by using examples from
> the works of (1) Haydn, (2) Mozart,
> and (3) Beethoven.

> With each order of twelve (12),
> enclose a check for two dollars
> ($2.00).

65. A place name which is not part of
an official name but is necessary in a
sentence is enclosed in parentheses:

> The Pittsburg (Kansas) Historical So-
> ciety should not be confused with
> the Pittsburgh (Pennsylvania) His-
> torical Society.

Brackets

66. Editorial comments or corrections are set off with brackets ([ ]):

> He said, "All those left [mostly women and children] should move back."

> D[j]akarta was our last stop.

67. Parenthetical material within parentheses is enclosed in brackets:

> After writing several novels (mostly about war experiences [such stories were quite popular]), he began writing plays.

Hyphen

The dictionary is an invaluable aid in all questions concerning hyphenation, and each specific use of a hyphen should be verified in the dictionary. This guide gives only general rules.

68. A hyphen (-) is used to divide a word at the end of a line when the word continues to the next line. Correct syllabication should always be observed:

> Joan tried hard to work the problems but failed.

69. A hyphen is used to form most compound words containing the following elements:

cross-eyed	single-pace
great-grandmother	double-edged
light-handed	ill-suited
heavy-laden	well-prepared

70. Hyphens are used between the words of a compound modifier when it precedes the noun but are usually omitted when the modifier follows the noun. Do not hyphenate a compound modifier with an adverb ending in *ly*.

He is a well-known author.
He is well known.
a word-for-word translation
The translation was word for word.
a tight-fitting sweater
a tightly fitting sweater

71. A hyphen is used to form compound nouns that show a combination of qualities or functions. Do not hyphenate chemical compounds:

secretary-treasurer
hydrogen peroxide

Chapter 11

FOREIGN TERMS

absence, in absentia (L.)
absurdity, to point of, ad absurdum (L.)
accomplished, accompli (Fr.)
account of, on, propter hoc (L.)
account, on, à compte (Fr.)
acquaintance, conocido (Sp.)
after, après (Fr.)
again; afresh, de nouveau (Fr.)
against, contra (L., Sp.)
age, edad (Sp.)
aged, viejo (Sp.)
aggressor, provocateur (Fr.)
agreed, d'accord (Fr.)
airmail, lentoposti (Finn.); par avion
    (Fr.); Flugpost (G); Luftpost (G.); por
    avión (Sp.)
alehouse, Bierhaus (G.)
almonds, with, amandine (Fr.)
amid, inter (L.)
among, inter alia (L.)
amount, importe (Sp.)
and, et (Fr.); und (G.); e (It.); y (Sp.)
anew, de novo (L.)
annexation, Anschluss (G.)
answer, please, R.S.V.P. (Fr.)

anti-Semitism, Judenhetze (G.)
anxiety, souci (Fr.)
apartment, Stube (G.)
appetite, appetit (Fr.)
apple cake, apelkaka (Sw.)
around; about, circum (L.)
association, Verein (G.)
attention!, achtung! (G.)
avenue, allée (Fr.); paseo (Sp.)
back to back, dos-à-dos (Fr.)
bad, mal (Fr., Sp.)
bad luck, malheur (Fr.)
bailiff, huissier (Fr.)
bakery, boulangerie (Fr.); forno (It.)
bank, Reichsbank (G.)
bar, Bierstube (G.)
bargain, à bon marché (Fr.)
basically, au fond (Fr.)
bay, bahía (Sp.)
beautiful, to kalon (Gr.); bello (Sp.)
beef, boeuf (Fr.); rosbif (Fr., Sp.); zrazy (Pol.)
beer, Bier (G.); bière (Fr.); birra (It.); cerveza (Sp.); öl (Sw.)
beerhouse, Bierhaus (G.)
before, antes (Sp.)
beginning, from the, ab initio (L.); ab ovo (L.)
beginning, in the, in principio (L.)
behind, après (Fr.)
behold the man, ecce homo (L.)
bell, Glocke (G.)
beloved, bien-aimé (Fr.); caro (It.); cher (Fr.); querido (Sp.)

below, infra (L.); sotto (It.)
below, as (stated), ut infra (L.)
besides; furthermore, además (Sp.)
better, best, mejor (Sp.)
between, inter alia (L.)
between ourselves, entre nous (Fr.)
between themselves, inter se (L.)
beverage, frappé (Fr.)
beware, cuidado (Sp.)
big, grande (It., Sp.)
bishop, obispo (Sp.)
blowfish, fugo (Jap.)
boarding school, pensionnat (Fr.)
body, corps (Fr.)
body of Christ, Corpus Christi (L.)
book, Buch (G.); libro (Sp.); livre (Fr.)
Bordeaux, of or from, bordelais (Fr.)
born, geboren (G.)
both, ambos (Sp.)
boy, muchacho (Sp.); garçon (Fr.)
brandy, Weinbrand (G.); acquavite
  (It.)
bread, Bauernbrot (lit.: farmer's bread)
  (G.); pain (Fr.); pan (Sp.); pane (It.);
  pão (Pg.)
breakfast, desayuno (Sp.); Frühstück
  (G.); petit déjeuner (Fr.)
broth, caldo (Sp.)
bull, toro (Sp.)
bullfighter, torero (Sp.)
bus, autobus (Fr., It.); autobús (Sp.)
butcher shop (pork), charcuterie (Fr.)
butter, burro (It.)
butterfly, papillon (Fr.)

bye and bye, in the, al-ki (Ind.)
by-pass, circonvallazione (It.); periférico (Mex. Sp.)
cabbage, kapusta (Pol., Russ.); cavolo (It.)
cake, gâteau (Fr.); torta (Sp.)
cake, coffee, Kaffeekuchen (G.)
call me, appellez-moi (Fr.)
cantor, hazah (Heb.)
carefree, sans souci (Fr.)
castle, Schloss (G.)
cauliflower, chou-fleur (Fr.)
celebrated, célèbre (Fr.)
certain, certo (It.)
certainly (yes), jawohl (G.)
cheerful, allegro (It.)
cheese, cacio (It.); formaggio (It.); fromage (Fr.); queijo (Pg.); queso (Sp.)
chicken, pollo (It., Sp.)
chickpea, garbanzo (Sp.)
child, niño (Sp.)
child, baby, baba (Hind.)
choir, coro (It.)
Christmas, Noël (Fr.); Navidad (Sp.)
Christmas Eve, Nochebuena (Sp.)
church, chiesa (It.); iglesia (Sp.)
cider, Apfelwein (G.)
citizen, citoyen (Fr.)
city, ciudad (Sp.); Stadt (G.)
club, Verein (G.)
codfish, bacalao (Sp.)
coin, a, moneda (Sp.)
cold, frío (Sp.); froid (Fr.)
come in, entrez (Fr.)

commander-in-chief, généralissime
  (Fr.)
commonly, vulgo (L.)
community, Gemeinschaft (G.)
companion, compadre (Sp.)
compassion, pietà (It.)
complete, accompli (Fr.)
conflict, culture, Kulturkampf (G.)
congeniality, Gemütlichkeit (G.)
contrary, on the, al contrario (Sp.)
corner, rincón (Sp.)
corporation, Sociedad Anónima (Abbr
  S.A.) (Sp.)
cost, prix (Fr.)
country, país (Sp.)
country, for one's, pro patria (L.)
countryman, paisano (Sp.)
countryside, campagne (Fr.)
course, of, parbleu (Fr.)
court, in, in curia (L.)
cove, ensenada (Sp.)
cow, vaca (Sp.)
craving, appétit (Fr.)
crew, cuadrilla (Sp.)
cuckold, cocu (Fr.)
cup, tasse (Fr.)
currency, dinero (Sp.)
cursed, sacré (Fr.)
damned, sacré (Fr.)
danger, danger (Fr.); Gefahr (G.); peli
  gro (Sp.); pericolo (It.)
darling, bien-aimé (Fr.)
dart, barbed, banderilla (Sp.)
date, from the, a dato (L.)

day, día (Sp.); Tag (G.)

day before yesterday, avant-hier (Fr.)

dear, caro (It.); cher (Fr.); querido (Sp.)

denial, désaveu (Fr.)

depths, out of, de profundis (L.)

died, obiit (L.)

dining room, comedor (Sp.)

dinner, dîner (Fr.)

disaster, malheur (Fr.)

discotheque, boite (Fr.)

discretion, at, à discrétion (Fr.)

dissenter (religious), Raskolnik (Russ.)

domestic state, in a, en famille (Fr.)

door, porta, portiera (It.); puerta (Sp.)

doubt, without, sans doute (Fr.)

down; underneath, abajo (Sp.)

drawing of the Virgin holding the body of Christ, Pietà (It.)

dreaming, Träumerei (G.)

drink, boisson (Fr.); bebida (Sp.)

duke, Herzog (G.)

East, este (Sp.)

Easter, Pâques (Fr.); Ostern (G.); Pascua (It., Sp.)

eggplant, moussaka (Gr.)

eminent, célèbre (Fr.)

end, to the, ad finem (L.)

enjoy the present, carpe diem (L.)

Enlightenment, the, Aufklärung (G.)

enough, bastante (Sp.)

entirely, tout à fait (Fr.); in toto (L.)

entrance, ticket, entrada (Sp.)

equality, égalité (Fr.)

era, edad (Sp.)

eunuch, castrato (It.)

evening, noche (Sp.)

everybody, tout le monde (Fr.)

everywhere, ubique (L.)

evil, mal (Fr., Sp.)

example, for, par exemple (Fr.); exempli gratia (Abbr., e.g.) (L.)

exclamation of amazement, caramba (Sp.)

excuse me, pardonnez-moi (Fr.); (mi) scusi (It.)

exit, salida (Sp.); sortie (Fr.)

expatriate, to, expatrier (Fr.)

expensive, caro (It.); cher (Fr.)

exploiter, cafajeste (Pg.)

extreme, to the, ad extremum (L.)

faithful, always, semper fidelis (L.)

famous, célèbre (Fr.)

Fascism, fascismo (It.)

father, pater (L.)

fault, my, mea culpa (L.)

fierce, farouche (Fr.)

finishing stroke, coup de grâce (Fr.)

fire, fuego (Sp.)

fish, fisk (Dan., Nor.); pesce (It.); poisson (Fr.); pez (Sp.)

fishing, pesca (Sp.)

flesh, carne (It., Sp.)

floats, pasos (Sp.)

floor, pavimento, piano (It.); andar (Pg.); piso (Sp.)

flower, fleur (Fr.)

flower arrangement, ikebana (Jap.)

follows, it, sequitur (abbr. *seq.*) (L.)

food, alimento (It., Sp.)

foot, on, à pied (Fr.)

force, fuerza (Sp.)

foreign, extranjero (Sp.); xenos (Gr.)

foreigner, étranger (Fr.)

forever, à jamais (Fr.); in perpetuum (L.)

forward, adelante (Sp.); en avant (Fr.)

frank, candide (Fr.); franco (It.)

frankfurter, Bockwurst (G.)

fresco, affresco (It.)

fried, chow (Chin.)

friend, as a, en ami (Fr.)

fritter, buñuelo (Sp.)

frost, ghiaccio (It.)

frozen, cold, helado (Sp.); gelé (Fr.)

fruit, Frucht (G.); fruta (Sp.); frutta (It.)

fruit, stewed, compote (Fr.)

frying pan, wok (Chin.)

furnished, garni (Fr.)

gait, allure (Fr.)

gambling, juego (Sp.)

garden, jardin (Fr.)

garlic, ail (Fr.); aglio (It.); ajo (Sp.)

geisha, kaesang (Kor.)

gentleman, gentilhomme (Fr.)

gin, genièvre (Fr.)

ginger, gingembre (Fr.)

girl, Mädchen (G.); muchacha (Sp.)

glass, glace (Fr.)

go away!, allez-vous-en! (Fr.)

go, lets!, Come on!, allons (Fr.)

good, bien (Fr.); buono (It.); bueno (Sp.)

good-by, auf Wiedersehen (G.); arrive-
derci, ciao, addio (It.); sayonara (Jap.);
adeus (Pg.)

good day, bonjour (Fr.)

good evening, bonsoir (Fr.)

good morning, bonjour (Fr.)

goose, Gans (G.)

grace of God, by, Dei gratia (L.)

grape, uva (It., Pg., Sp.)

gratuity, pourboise (Fr.); Trinkgeld
(G.); bonamano (It.); propina (Sp.)

gravy, jus (Fr.)

great, grande (It., Sp.)

greatly, di molto (It.); muy (Sp.)

group, en bloc (Fr.)

guard, on, en garde (Fr.)

guerilla fighters, fedayeen (Ar.)

guilt, culpa (L.)

gypsy, gitano (Sp.)

hail, heil (G.); hoch (G.)

hail, victory!, Sieg Heil (G.)

half, à demi (Fr.)

ham, jambon (Fr.); prosciutto (It.);
jamón (Sp.)

handicraft, Handwerk (G.)

handmade, handgeschöpft (G.)

happily, heureusement (Fr.)

happy, feliz (Sp.)

harmony, concordia (Sp.)

head, capo (It.)

health, to your, slàinte (Gael.); la'chaim
(Heb.)

hello; How goes it?, wie geht's? (G.);
ciao (It.); hola (Sp.)

helmet, spiked, Pickelhaube (G.)
help!, socorro (Sp.)
hen, poule, poulette (Fr.)
here lies, ci-gît (Fr.)
high, haut (Fr.)
highest, in the; on high, in excelsis (L.)
highness, altesse (Fr.)
highway, Strasse (G.); carretera, camino (Sp.)
himself; herself; itself, sí (Sp.)
history, Geschichte (G.)
hog, maiale (It.)
holy, sacré (Fr.)
homesickness, Heimweh (G.)
honor, honneur (Fr.)
horse, caballo (Sp.)
horseback, on, a caballo (Sp.); à cheval (Fr.)
horseman (bullfight), picador (Sp.)
hot; heat, chaud (Fr.); caldo (It.); caliente (Sp.)
hotel, Gasthof (G.); albergo (It.); parador (Sp.)
housewife, Hausfrau (G.)
how much? how many?, ¿cuánto? (Sp.)
huh, hein (Fr.)
hush!, chut (Fr.)
ice; frost, ghiaccio (It.); hielo (Sp.)
ice cream, glace (Fr.); helado (Sp.)
incredible, incroyable (Fr.)
indeed, wohl (G.)
informally, en famille (Fr.)

inn, auberge (Fr.); Gasthaus (G.); osteria (It.); pousada (Pg.); posada, fonda (Sp.)

inside, adentro (Sp.)

intelligence, cervelle (Fr.)

isn't it?, ¿verdad? (Sp.)

jail, calabozo (Sp.)

jelly, gelée (Fr.)

Jesus, Gesù (It.)

journey, viaje (Sp.)

joy, allégresse (Fr.)

judgment of God, judicium Dei (L.)

juniper, genièvre (Fr.)

just, à point (Fr.)

king, rey (Sp.)

know-how, jeito (Pg.)

lady, Frau (G.); sahibah (Hind.); pani (Pol.); donna (It.)

lagoon, laguna (Sp.)

lake, lago (It., Pg., Sp.)

lamb, cordero (Sp.)

language, lengua (Sp.)

last, último (Sp.)

last, at, enfin (Fr.); alfine (It.)

lavatory, lavabo (Fr., Sp.)

lawyer, abogado (Sp.)

leadership, Führerschaft (G.)

learned, sabio (Sp.)

least, menos (Sp.)

left, to (on) the, à gauche (Fr.)

leggings, chaparreras (Sp.)

legislature, Reichstag (G.)

lemonade, citronnade (Fr.)

Lent, carême (Fr.)

less, menos (Sp.)
letter, lettre (Fr.)
library, bibliothèque (Fr.)
life, vida (Sp.)
light bulb, bombilla (Sp.)
light of the world, lux mundi (L.)
liking, gré (Fr.)
little, a, un poco (It., Sp.); pequeño (Sp.)
liver, foie (Fr.); hígado (Sp.); Leber
  (G.)
living space, Lebensraum (G.)
loaf, pane (It.); pão (Pg.); pain (Fr.);
  pan, torta (Sp.)
lodging, albergue (Pg., Sp.)
long live, vivat (L.)
love, amore (It.)
lover, amant (Fr.); amante (It., Sp.)
luckily, heureusement (Fr.)
lunch, déjeuner (Fr.); almôço (Pg.);
  almuerzo (Sp.)
lunchmeat, charcuterie (Fr.)
madame, dona (Pg.)
madman, aliéné (Fr.)
maiden, Mädchen (G.)
mail, correo (Sp.)
maize, maíz (Sp.)
make-shift, pis-aller (Fr.)
male, macho (Sp.)
man, good-natured, bonhomme (Fr.)
man of the house, Hausherr (G.)
manner (custom) of, more (L.)
manner, in the, ad modum (L.)
mannerism, allure (Fr.)
manor house, Herrenhaus (G.)

marketplace, plaza (Sp.); halle (Fr.)

martial art, aikido (Jap.); Tae Kwon Do (Kor.); Taichi (Chin.)

master race, Herrenvolk (G.)

match, a, allumette (Fr.)

mat, straw, tatami (Jap.)

meal, repas (Fr.); comida (Sp.)

meat, viande (Fr.); carne (It., Sp.); churrasco (Sp.)

melted, fondu (Fr.)

menu, cardápio (Pg.)

mercy, pietà (It.)

Mexican-American, chicano (Sp.)

might, fuerza (Sp.)

migration of nations, Völkerwanderung (G.)

mind, of sound, compos mentis (L.)

military force, Reichswehr (G.)

milk, lait, (Fr.); latte (It.); leche (Sp.)

mint, menthe (Fr.)

misfortune, malheur (Fr.)

mistake, malentendu (Fr.)

mister, pan (Pol.)

misunderstanding, malentendu (Fr.)

monastery (or convent), convento (Sp.)

monetary unit, Reichsmark (G.); peso (Sp.)

money, plata, dinero (Sp.)

month, mes (Sp.)

moon, lune (Fr.); luna (It., Sp.)

morality, Sittlichkeit (G.)

most, más (Sp.)

mother, madre (Sp.)

mountain, montaña (Sp.)

mountain range, serra (Pg.); serranía (Sp.)

mouth, boca (Sp.)

much, beaucoup (Fr.); mucho (Sp.)

much, too, de trop (Fr.); troppo (It.); demasiado (Sp.)

museum, art, pinakothek (G.)

mushroom, fungo (It.)

mutton, mouton (Fr.); castrato (It.)

name, nombre (Sp.)

name, in the, in nomine (L.)

nation, país (Sp.)

new, nuevo (Sp.)

night, noche (Sp.)

no, non (Fr.); nein (G.)

noodles, galuska (Hung.); fettuccine (It.)

north, norte (Sp.)

obligation, religious, mitzvah (Heb.)

observation, Anschauung (G.)

October festival, Oktoberfest (G.)

office, ufficio (It.); sala (Pg.)

oil, huile (Fr.); olio (It.); aceite (Sp.)

old (person), viejo (Sp.)

onion soup, Zwiebel suppe (G.)

open, ouvert (Fr.); abierto (Sp.)

orange, naranja (Sp.)

organ grinder, Leierkastenmann (G.)

oven, forno (It.)

ox, bue (It.)

pain, Schmerz (G.); dolor (Sp.)

painting, kakemono (Jap.)

palace, palazzo (It.)

pancakes, crêpes (Fr.); blini (Russ.)

pants, underwear, bragas (Sp.)

pardon me, pardonnez-moi (Fr.); (mi) scusi (It.)

parliament, Reichsrat (G.)

part, in, partim (L.)

partial payment, à compte (Fr.)

partly, partim (L.)

passenger, viajero (Sp.)

pastry, pâtissèrie (Fr.); knish (Heb.); kringle (Nor.); pączki (Pol.); baklava (Turk.)

patented, breveté (Fr.)

pauper, pobre (Sp.)

payment, abonnement (Fr.)

peace, pax (L.); paz (Sp.)

peace be with you, pax vobiscum (L.); salaam aleikum (Ar.)

peace, in, in pace (L.)

peas, green, petit pois (Fr.)

pencil, lapis (It.)

people, gente (It., Sp.)

percent, por ciento (Sp.)

perfection, ne plus ultra (L.)

perfume, parfum (Fr.)

peripheral, periférico (Sp.)

photographers, paparazzi (It.)

pig, porc (Fr.); maiale (It.)

pilaf, pilau (Fr.)

pineapple, piña (Sp.)

pine cone, piña (Sp.)

pity, pietà (It.)

place, in, in loco (L.)

plain, a, llano (Sp.)

plainsman, llanero (Sp.)

plantation, coffee, cafetal (Sp.)

play, juego (Sp.)

please, s'il vous plaît (Fr.); bitte (G.); per favore (It.); por favor (Sp.)

pleasure, at, a piacere (It.)

point of view, Anschauung (G.)

police, Polizei (G.); polizia (It.); policia (Sp.)

police, bar (Oktoberfest), Bierstubepolizei (G.)

police (elite), Schutzstaffel (abbr. S.S.) (G.)

policy, eastern, Ostpolitik (G.)

policy, international, Weltpolitik (G.)

politician, politico (Sp.)

poor, pobre (Sp.)

poor man's stew, puchero (Sp.)

pork, porc (Fr.); maiale (It.)

postage free, franco (It.)

post office, correo (Sp.)

post office box, Postfach (G.)

pound, livre (Fr.)

power, fuerza (Sp.)

power (a nation's), Weltmacht (G.)

pretty, bellino (It.); bonito (Sp.)

price, prix (Fr.); precio (Sp.)

prison, calabozo (Sp.)

privately, in camera (L.)

prize, prix (Fr.); premio (It.)

prize, great, grand prix (Fr.)

pun, calembour (Fr.)

purpose, on, à dessein (Fr.)

purser, boursier (Fr.)

queen, regina (L.)
quick, schnell (G.)
railroad, Eisenbahn (G.); ferrocarril
 (Sp.)
rain, lluvia (Sp.)
rainbow, arc-en-ciel (Fr.)
rapid, schnell (G.)
refreshment, refresco (Sp.)
regarding, in re (L.)
reminder, aide-mémoire (Fr.)
residence, pied-à-terre (Fr.)
restaurant, Gasthaus, Ratskeller (G.)
reverie, Träumerei (G.)
reward, prix (Fr.); premio (It.)
rice, arroz (Sp.)
rifleman, tirailleur (Fr.)
right, à point (Fr.)
right, to the, à droite (Fr.)
river, río (Sp.)
road, camino, carretera (Sp.)
roast, rôti (Fr.); asado (Sp.)
robe, jelbaba (Ar.)
Roman peace, Pax Romana (L.)
room, Stube (G.); sala (Pg.)
royal, real (Sp.)
sacred, sacré (Fr.)
sage, rishi (Skr.)
salt, with a grain of, cum grano salis
 (L.)
Santa Claus, Père Noël (Fr.); Befana
 (It.)
sauerkraut, choucroute (Fr.)
sausage, link, Bratwurst (G.)

sausage, liver, Braunschweiger, Leber-
wurst (G.)

sausage, pork, Blutwurst (G.); chorizo
(Sp.)

school, école, lycée (Fr.); heder, yeshiva
(Heb.)

sea, mar (Sp.); mer (Fr.)

seasickness, mal de mer (Fr.)

seer, rishni (Skr.)

see you soon, à bientôt (Fr.)

seize the day, carpe diem (L.)

seizure (of government), coup d'état
(Fr.)

sheep, mouton (Fr.)

shellfish, fruits de mer (Fr.)

shelter, albergue (Pg., Sp.)

sherry, jerez (Sp.); xérès (Fr.)

sidesaddle, galápago (Sp.)

silver, plata (Sp.)

simple (person), ingénu (Fr.)

sincerely, ex animo (L.)

**slab, stone (for grinding corn and
maize),** metate (Sp.)

slowly, despacio (Sp.)

slum, favela (Pg.)

sly, farouche (Fr.)

small, pequeño (Sp.)

smell, odeur (Fr.)

smoked, fumé (Fr.)

snail, escargot (Fr.)

snow, nieve (Sp.)

snow-covered, nevado (Sp.)

society, Gesellschaft (G.)

softly, piano (It.)

sorrow, dolor (Sp.)

sorrowful, addolorato (It.)

south, sud (Fr., Sp.); sur (Sp.)

Spain, España (Sp.)

spirit, Geist (G.)

spirit of the world, the, Weltgeist (G.)

spite of, in, malgré (Fr.)

sport, juego (Sp.)

squires, young, Junkerschaft (G.)

SS (secret police), Schutzstaffel (G.)

star, étoile (Fr.)

state, état (Fr.)

steak, tournedos (Fr.)

step, pas (Fr.)

stew, stufato (It.)

stone, a, lapis (L.)

stop it! that's enough!, basta (It.)

stop thief!, au voleur (Fr.)

storm troops, Sturmabteilung (abbr. S.A.) (G.)

story (of a building), étage (Fr.)

stranger, étranger (Fr.); xenos (Gr.); extranjero (Sp.)

street, rue (Fr.); katu (Finn.); Strasse (G.); calle (Sp.)

strength, fuerza (Sp.)

study, étude (Fr.)

subscription, abonnement (Fr.)

suburbs, banlieue (Fr.)

subway, Untergrundbahn (G.)

successfully, heureusement (Fr.)

sudden, schnell (G.)

suffering, Schmerz (G.)

sugar, sucre (Fr.)

sun, soleil (Fr.); sol (Sp.)

superhighway, autostrada (It.); auto-pista (Sp.)

superman, a, Übermensch (G.)

supper, avondeten (D.); dîner (Fr.); cena (Sp.)

sure! (to be), ma foi (Fr.); certo (It.)

surround, gherao (Hind.)

swastika, Hakenkreuz (G.)

sweetheart, amant (Fr.); Mädchen (G.)

talk, parle (Fr.); habla (Sp.)

tapestry, kilim (Pol.)

taproom, Bierstube (G.)

tavern, Heuriger (G.)

tea, té (Sp.)

tea (South American), maté (Sp.)

temporarily, ad interim (L.)

thanks (be) to God, Deo gratias (l.)

thanks (many), vielen Dank (G.); merci beaucoup (Fr.)

thank you, arigato (Jap.); dankeschön (G.); merci, (Fr.); gracias (Sp.)

that is, id est (abbr. i.e.) (L.)

that is to say, das heisst (G.)

therefore, ergo (L.)

there it is, voilà (Fr.)

thoroughfare, corso (It.)

thought, pensée (Fr.)

throne, from the, ex cathedra (L.)

time flies, tempus fugit (L.)

tip, bonamano (It.); pourboire (Fr.); propina (Sp.); Trinkgeld (G.)

toast, a drinking, brindisi (It.)

toasted, tostado (Sp.)

tobacco, tabac (Fr.)

tomorrow, until, à demain (Fr.)

tongue, lengua (Sp.)

tortoise (freshwater), galápago (Sp.)

toughness, machismo (Sp.)

town, Stadt (G.)

town hall, ayuntamiento (Sp.)

traveler, viajero (Sp.)

tree, árbol (Sp.)

trip, viaje (Sp.)

trouble, souci (Fr.)

trouble-free, sans souci (Fr.)

troublemaker, provocateur (Fr.)

trousers, bombachas (Sp.)

truth, verité (Fr.); Wahrheit (G.); veritas (L.); pravda (Russ.)

turkey, tacchino (It.); dinde (Fr.); pavo (Sp.)

Twilight of the Gods, Götter-dämmerung (G.)

two, for, à deux (Fr.)

typist, dactylographe (Fr.)

under, sotto (It.)

underneath, abajo (Sp.)

under study (consideration), ad referendum (L.)

unexpected, imprévu (Fr.)

union, Anschluss (G.)

United States of America, Etats-Unis (Fr.)

unrestricted, à discrétion (Fr.)

unsurpassable, ne plus ultra (L.)

until, hasta (Sp.)
uplifted, haut (Fr.)
upper, haut (Fr.)
useless (a "lemon"), abacaxi (Pg.)
usher, huissier (Fr.)
veal, vitèllo (It.)
very, muy (Sp.)
very (much), très (Fr.)
very well, très bien (Fr.)
village, aldea (Sp.)
vineyard, viña (Sp.)
virility, machismo (Sp.)
virtue, honneur, virtu (Fr.)
visit, séjour (Fr.)
voice, vox (L.)
vow, by, ex voto (L.)
Wait!, Attendez! (Fr.)
waiter, garçon (Fr.)
walk, paseo (Sp.)
war, guerra (Sp.)
warfare, Krieg (G)
watchtower, atalaya (Sp.)
water, acqua (It.); eau (Fr.);
  vand (Dan.); vann (Nor.); vatten
  (Sw.)
way, by the, obiter (L.)
Way of the Cross, Via Crucis (L.)
weight, peso (Sp.)
welcome, benvenuto (It.)
welcome, (you're), de nada (Sp.)
west, oeste (Sp.)
whip, chicote (Sp.)
Whither thou goest, quo vadis (L.)
wife, Frau (G.)

will, at, à discrétion (Fr.)
window, glace (Fr.)
wine, vin (Fr., Scand.)
wine (light red), clairet (Fr.)
wine (port), oporto (Pg.)
wine (red, fruit), sangría (Sp.)
wise, sabio (Sp.)
within, from, ab intra (L.)
wolf, lobo (Sp.)
woman, femme (Fr.); Frau (G.); mujer (Sp.)
woman of ill-repute, demi-mondaine (Fr.)
woman (of the house), Hausfrau (G.)
woods, bois (Fr.)
work out well, it will, ça ira (Fr.)
world, mundo (Sp.)
world-wide, mundial (Sp.)
worry, souci (Fr.)
year, an (Fr.); año (Sp.)
year of Christ, in the, anno Christi (L.)
yes, ja (G.); oui (Fr.); sì (It.); sí (Sp.)
yes, indeed, jawohl (G.)
yesterday, ayer (Sp.)
you, vous (Fr.); usted (Sp.)

METRIC SYSTEM

Linear Measure

Unit	U.S. equivalent
square millimeter (mm²)	0.00155 square inch
square centimeter (cm²)	0.155 square inch
centare (ca) or square meter (m²)	10.76 square feet
deciare (da)	11.96 square yards
aretare (a) or square dekameter (dkm²)	119.60 square yards
dekare (dka)	0.247 acre
hectare (ha) or square hectometer (hm²)	2.471 acres
square kilometer (km²)	0.386 square mile

Area

Unit	U.S. equivalent
micron (μ)	0.00003937 inch, 0.03937 mil
millimeter (mm)	0.03937 inch, 39.37 mils
centimeter (cm)	0.3937 inch
decimeter (dm)	3.937 inches
meter (m)	39.37 inches
dekameter (dkm)	10.93 yards, 32.81 feet
hectometer (hm)	109.36 yards, 328.1 feet
kilometer (km)	0.6214 mile

Capacity

Unit	U.S. equivalent dry	U.S. equivalent liquid
milliliter (ml)	0.0018 pint	0.034 fluidounce
centiliter (cl)	0.018 pint	0.338 fluidounce
deciliter (dl)	0.18 pint	3.381 fluidounces
liter (l)	0.908 quart	1.057 quarts
dekaliter (dkl)	1.14 pecks	2.643 gallons
hectoliter (hl)	2.84 bushels	26.425 gallons
kiloliter (kl)	28.38 bushels	264.25 gallons

METRIC SYSTEM

Volume

Unit	U.S. equivalent
cubic millimeter (mm³)	0.000061 cubic inch, 0.016 minim
cubic centimeter (cm³ or cc)	0.061 cubic inch
cubic decimeter (dm³)	61.02 cubic inches
decistere (ds)	3.53 cubic feet
stere (s) or cubic meter (m³)	1.308 cubic yards, 35.31 cubic feet
dekastere (dks)	13.079 cubic yards
cubic dekameter (dkm³)	1,307.943 cubic yards

Mass and Weight

Unit	U.S. equivalent (*Avoirdupois weight*)
milligram (mg)	0.0154 grain
centigram (cg)	0.154 grain
decigram (dg)	1.543 grains
gram (g or gm)	0.0353 ounce, 15.43 grains
dekagram (dkg)	0.353 ounce
hectogram (hg)	3.527 ounces
kilogram (kg)	2.205 pounds
metric ton (MT or t)	1.102 tons, 2,204.6 pounds

UNIT		
		Avoirdupois
short ton		20 short hundredweight, 2000 lbs.
long ton		20 long hundredweight, 2240 lbs.
short hundredweight		100 lbs., 0.05 short tons
long hundredweight		112 lbs., 0.05 long tons
pound (lb.)	**WEIGHT**	16 oz., 7000 gr.
ounce (oz.)		16 drams, 437.5 gr.
pennyweight		
dram		27.343 gr., 0.0625 oz.
scruple		
grain (gr.)		0.036 drams, 0.002285 oz.
		U.S. liquid measure
bushel		
peck		
gallon		4 quarts (231 in.^{3})
quart	**CAPACITY**	2 pints (57.75 in.^{3})
pint		4 gills (28.875 in.^{3})
gill		4 fluidounces (7.218 in.^{3})
fluidounce		8 fluidrams (1.804 in.^{3})
fluidram		60 minims (0.225 in.^{3})
minim		1/60 fluidram (0.003759 in.^{3})
		Volume
cubic yard		27 ft.^{3}, 46,656 in.^{3}
cubic foot		1728 in.^{3}, 0.0370 yd.^{3}
cubic inch		0.00058 ft.^{3}, 0.000021 yd.^{3}
square mile		
acre		
square rod		
square yard	**DIMENSION**	
square foot		
square inch		
mile		
rod		
yard		
foot		
inch		

UNIT		
		Troy
short ton		
long ton		
short hundredweight		
long hundredweight		
pound (lb.)	**WEIGHT**	12 oz., 240 pennyweight, 5760 gr.
ounce (oz.)		20 pennyweight, 480 gr.
pennyweight		24 gr., 0.05 oz.
dram		
scruple		
grain (gr.)		0.042 pennyweight, 0.002083 oz.
		U.S. dry measure
bushel		4 pecks (2150.42 in.^{3})
peck		8 quarts (537.605 in.^{3})
gallon		
quart	**CAPACITY**	2 pints (67.200 in.^{3})
pint		$\frac{1}{2}$ quart (33.600 in.^{3})
gill		
fluidounce		
fluidram		
minim		
		Area
cubic yard		
cubic foot		
cubic inch		
square mile		640 acres, 102,400 rods^2
acre		4840 yd.^{2}, 43,560 ft.^{2}
square rod	**DIMENSION**	30.25 yd.^{2}, 0.006 acres
square yard		1296 in.^{2}, 9 ft.^{2}
square foot		144 in.^{2}, 0.111 yd.^{2}
square inch		0.007 ft.^{2}, 0.00077 yd.^{2}
mile		
rod		
yard		
foot		
inch		

UNIT		
		Apothecaries'
short ton		
long ton		
short hundredweight		
long hundredweight	**WEIGHT**	
pound (lb.)		12 oz., 5760 gr.
ounce (oz.)		8 drams, 480 gr.
pennyweight		
dram		3 scruples, 60 gr.
scruple		20 gr., 0.333 drams
grain (gr.)		0.05 scruples, 0.002083 oz.
		British liquid and dry measure
bushel		4 pecks (2219.36 in.^{3})
peck		2 gallons (554.84 in.^{3})
gallon		4 quarts (277.420 in.^{3})
quart	**CAPACITY**	2 pints (69.355 in.^{3})
pint		4 gills (34.678 in.^{3})
gill		5 fluidounces (8.669 in.^{3})
fluidounce		8 fluidrams (1.7339 in.^{3})
fluidram		60 minims (0.216734 in.^{3})
minim		1/60 fluidram (0.003612 in.^{3})
		Length
cubic yard		
cubic foot		
cubic inch		
square mile		
acre		
square rod	**DIMENSION**	
square yard		
square foot		
square inch		
mile		320 rods, 1760 yd., 5280 ft.
rod		5.50 yd., 16.5 ft.
yard		3 ft., 36 in.
foot		12 in., 0.333 yd.
inch		0.083 ft., 0.027 yd.

TABLE OF SQUARES, CUBES, SQUARE ROOTS, AND CUBE ROOTS

No.	Square	Cube	Square Root	Cube Root
1	1	1	1.000	1.000
2	4	8	1.414	1.260
3	9	27	1.732	1.442
4	16	64	2.000	1.587
5	25	125	2.236	1.710
6	36	216	2.449	1.817
7	49	343	2.646	1.913
8	64	512	2.828	2.000
9	81	729	3.000	2.080
10	100	1,000	3.162	2.154
11	121	1,331	3.317	2.224
12	144	1,728	3.464	2.289
13	169	2,197	3.606	2.351
14	196	2,744	3.742	2.410
15	225	3,375	3.873	2.466
16	256	4,096	4.000	2.520
17	289	4,913	4.123	2.571
18	324	5,832	4.243	2.621
19	361	6,859	4.359	2.668
20	400	8,000	4.472	2.714
21	441	9,261	4.583	2.759
22	484	10,648	4.690	2.802
23	529	12,167	4.796	2.844

No.	Square	Cube	Square Root	Cube Root
24	576	13,824	4.899	2.884
25	625	15,625	5.000	2.924
26	676	17,576	5.099	2.962
27	729	19,683	5.196	3.000
28	784	21,952	5.292	3.037
29	841	24,389	5.385	3.072
30	900	27,000	5.477	3.107
31	961	29,791	5.568	3.141
32	1,024	32,768	5.657	3.175
33	1,089	35,937	5.745	3.208
34	1,156	39,304	5.831	3.240
35	1,225	42,875	5.916	3.271
36	1,296	46,656	6.000	3.302
37	1,369	50,653	6.083	3.332
38	1,444	54,872	6.164	3.362
39	1,521	59,319	6.245	3.391
40	1,600	64,000	6.325	3.420
41	1,681	68,921	6.403	3.448
42	1,764	74,088	6.481	3.476
43	1,849	79,507	6.557	3.503
44	1,936	85,184	6.633	3.530
45	2,025	91,125	6.708	3.557
46	2,116	97,336	6.782	3.583
47	2,209	103,823	6.856	3.609
48	2,304	110,592	6.928	3.634
49	2,401	117,649	7.000	3.659
50	2,500	125,000	7.071	3.684
51	2,601	132,651	7.141	3.708

No.	Square	Cube	Square Root	Cube Root
52	2,704	140,608	7.211	3.732
53	2,809	148,877	7.280	3.756
54	2,916	157,464	7.348	3.780
55	3,025	166,375	7.416	3.803
56	3,136	175,616	7.483	3.826
57	3,249	185,193	7.550	3.848
58	3,364	195,112	7.616	3.871
59	3,481	205,379	7.681	3.893
60	3,600	216,000	7.746	3.915
61	3,721	226,981	7.810	3.936
62	3,844	238,328	7.874	3.958
63	3,969	250,047	7.937	3.979
64	4,096	262,144	8.000	4.000
65	4,225	274,625	8.062	4.021
66	4,356	287,496	8.124	4.041
67	4,489	300,763	8.185	4.061
68	4,624	314,432	8.246	4.082
69	4,761	328,509	8.307	4.101
70	4,900	343,000	8.367	4.121
71	5,041	357,911	8.426	4.141
72	5,184	373,248	8.485	4.160
73	5,329	389,017	8.544	4.179
74	5,476	405,224	8.602	4.198
75	5,625	421,875	8.660	4.217
76	5,776	438,976	8.718	4.236
77	5,929	456,533	8.775	4.254
78	6,084	474,552	8.832	4.273
79	6,241	493,039	8.888	4.291
80	6,400	512,000	8.944	4.309

No.	Square	Cube	Square Root	Cube Root
81	6,561	531,441	9.000	4.327
82	6,724	551,368	9.055	4.344
83	6,889	571,787	9.110	4.362
84	7,056	592,704	9.165	4.379
85	7,225	614,125	9.219	4.397
86	7,396	636,056	9.274	4.414
87	7,569	658,503	9.327	4.431
88	7,744	681,472	9.381	4.448
89	7,921	704,969	9.434	4.465
90	8,100	729,000	9.487	4.481
91	8,281	753,571	9.539	4.498
92	8,464	778,688	9.592	4.514
93	8,649	804,357	9.644	4.531
94	8,836	830,584	9.695	4.547
95	9,025	857,375	9.747	4.563
96	9,216	884,736	9.798	4.579
97	9,409	912,673	9.849	4.595
98	9,604	941,192	9.899	4.610
99	9,801	970,299	9.950	4.626
100	10,000	1,000,000	10.000	4.642

INDEX

INDEX